What the Bible Says about the Dangers of Self-Deception

What the Bible Says about the Dangers of Self-Deception

An Exegetical Approach

JOSEPH K. PAK

WIPF & STOCK · Eugene, Oregon

WHAT THE BIBLE SAYS ABOUT THE DANGERS OF SELF-DECEPTION
An Exegetical Approach

Copyright © 2024 Joseph K. Pak. All rights reserved. Except for brief quotations in critical publications or reviews, no part of this book may be reproduced in any manner without prior written permission from the publisher. Write: Permissions, Wipf and Stock Publishers, 199 W. 8th Ave., Suite 3, Eugene, OR 97401.

Wipf & Stock
An Imprint of Wipf and Stock Publishers
199 W. 8th Ave., Suite 3
Eugene, OR 97401

www.wipfandstock.com

PAPERBACK ISBN: 979-8-3852-2711-2
HARDCOVER ISBN: 979-8-3852-2712-9
EBOOK ISBN: 979-8-3852-2713-6

10/14/24

Unless otherwise noted, Scripture is from The ESV® Bible (The Holy Bible, English Standard Version®). ESV® Text Edition: 2016. Copyright © 2001 by Crossway, a publishing ministry of Good News Publishers. The ESV® text has been reproduced in cooperation with and by permission of Good News Publishers. Unauthorized reproduction of this publication is prohibited. All rights reserved.

Where noted, Scripture is from THE HOLY BIBLE, NEW INTERNATIONAL VERSION®, NIV® Copyright © 1973, 1978, 1984, 2011 by Biblica, Inc.® Used by permission. All rights reserved worldwide.

Where noted, Scripture is from the PHILLIPS MODERN ENGLISH BIBLE, by J. B. Phillips, "The New Testament in Modern English", Copyright© 1962 edition, published by HarperCollins.

Contents

1	Introduction	1
2	Self-Deception in Philosophy, Theology, and Psychology	5
3	Self-Deception in the Old Testament	14
4	Self-Deception in the New Testament	55
5	So What?	125
6	Summary	133
	Bibliography	145

1

Introduction

WHAT IS SELF-DECEPTION? WE use various expressions to describe self-deception: "He keeps telling himself the same old lie," "She rejects the truth, even though it is clear she recognizes it," "He intentionally misleads himself," "He doesn't know because he doesn't want to know," "She deliberately closes her eyes to the evidence," etc.[1] Self-deception can be expressed in different ways: "The self-deceived say one thing but do another; they entertain one thought, but dispositionally believe otherwise; they attribute one belief to themselves, but actually have another; they avoid one kind of evidence and seek out another; they consciously believe one thing and unconsciously believe another."[2] I hope you are beginning to think that self-deception is not such an unfamiliar phenomenon.

Self-deception is not a strange notion to the biblical writers. John says, "If we say we have no sin, we deceive ourselves, and the truth is not in us" (1 John 1:8). Paul warns his readers not to be deceived about who can inherit eternal life (1 Cor 6:9, 10; Gal 6:7–8). James says someone who believes himself to be religious but does not control his tongue "deceives his own heart" (Jas 1:26). According to Via, "Both Paul and Matthew see human beings as enmeshed in a self-deception that promotes a cover

---

1. Alton, "Morality of Self-Deception," 141.
2. Funkhouser, *Self-Deception*, 128.

story of righteousness in order to conceal a real story of unrighteousness (Gal 6:3; Phil 3:6–10; Rom 9:30—10:3; Matt 23:25–28)."[3]

Plantinga describes self-deception this way:

> Self-deception is a shadowy phenomenon by which we pull the wool over some part of our own psyche. We put a move on ourselves. We deny, suppress, or minimize what we know to be true. We assert, adorn, and elevate what we know to be false. We prettify ugly realities and sell ourselves the prettified versions. Thus a liar might transform "I tell a lot of lies to shore up my pride" to "Occasionally, I finesse the truth in order to spare other people's feelings." We become our own dupes, playing the role of both perpetrator and victim. We know the truth—and yet we do not know it, because we persuade ourselves of its opposite.[4]

Perhaps we can agree that self-deception is something that we are all guilty of to one degree or another.

In fact, according to Ten Elshof, self-deception is one of the most distinguishing marks of humanity, and "historically, few masters of Christian spirituality have failed to notice the significance of self-deception. Christian thinkers through the ages have had a special interest in the bearing of self-deception on the Christian life and the pursuit of—or flight from—God, and it has long served as a key element in the explanation of sin, moral failure, and the avoidance of God."[5] Self-deception is also related to a wide variety of phenomena such as irrationality, wishful thinking, delusions, imperfect memory, ignorance, avoidance, hypocrisy, maintenance of self-respect, and false belief.[6]

Benjamin Franklin once quipped, "Who has deceived thee so often as thyself?"[7] It is a fundamental experience and the starting point of philosophy since Socrates.[8] Self-deception is thought to play a role in the medical world, the financial world, environmental legislation, politics, religion, and even in air crashes, warfare, and terrorism.[9] Ten Elshof notes, "Philosophers, social scientists, and psychologists have long been aware of the

---

3. Via, *Self-Deception and Wholeness*, 133.
4. Plantinga, *Not the Way*, 105.
5. Ten Elshof, *I Told Me So*, 5.
6. Botha, "Theology, Rationality and Truth-Claims," 101.
7. Bahnsen, "Crucial Concept of Self-Deception," 10.
8. Hållén, "Different Kind of Ignorance," 106.
9. Dings, "Social Strategies in Self-Deception," 21.

pervasive reality of self-deception. For centuries, it has been called upon to explain various forms of irrationality and dysfunction."[10]

Psychologists consider self-deception a ubiquitous phenomenon and view virtually all humans as constantly hiding the truth from themselves.[11] What are its harmful effects on individuals, communities, Christendom, and the world? Why is it so deeply embedded in the human psyche both individually and corporately? Self-deception is an important and pervasive topic repeatedly warned against in the Bible. Proper attention to self-deception is necessary to prevent it from leading to fatal results. Karl Barth noted that self-deception would lead to self-destruction.[12]

I have researched the topic of self-deception off and on for more than two decades. In my articles "Self-Deception in Current Philosophical Discussions and Its Importance in Theology"[13] and "Self-Deception in Theology,"[14] I examined self-deception in philosophy and theology. In this book, I will conduct an exegetical study of some biblical passages that address self-deception with the aid of philosophical and theological insights toward the goal of presenting a coherent picture of what the Bible teaches about self-deception—what it is, why it happens, what its consequences are, and how to deal with it. Though much has been written on the topic of self-deception from philosophical, psychological, and theological perspectives, much work is still needed in exegetical studies of the biblical passages that address this important topic.

The Scripture teaches that self-deception is a failure to know ourselves accurately (the opposite of self-knowledge), is closely related to sin, stems from pride and selfish desires, and prevents people from knowing and loving God.[15] Self-deception causes sinners to create God in their own image and reject the one true God. In this way, those who do not know God or even oppose him can consider themselves deeply religious. It is very troubling to hear Jesus say that on the day of his second coming, he will say, "I never knew you" to those who protest that he should let them into his

---

10. Ten Elshof, *I Told Me So*, 5.
11. Botha, "Theology, Rationality and Truth-Claims," 101.
12. Barth, *Church Dogmatics*, 143–44.
13. Pak, "Self-Deception in Current," 13–21.
14. Pak, "Self-Deception in Theology," 405–16.
15. Self-deception may involve deceiving ourselves about someone or something other than ourselves, but even in those cases failure of self-knowledge is still involved in that we are failing to know about what we know—a failure of accurate self-assessment.

kingdom, reminding him that they have done impressive ministry deeds all in his name (Matt 7:21–23). Tragically, Jesus says there will be many people on that day who make such a claim, and, as I will discuss later, this seems to be one example of self-deception in the Bible.

In chapter 2 of this book, I will share what philosophers, theologians, and psychologists think about self-deception and glean insights from them so they can shed light on our interpretation of the Bible. Chapters 3 and 4 are the central part of the book where we will examine many of the passages in the Bible that mention or are related to the topic of self-deception. In chapter 5, we will raise some questions about the benefits and strategies of self-deception and how to overcome its harmful effects. Then chapter 6 will provide a summary of our interpretation of each of the passages in chapters 3 and 4 for a quick reference.

2

Self-Deception in Philosophy, Theology, and Psychology

SELF-DECEPTION IN PHILOSOPHY

SELF-DECEPTION HAS BEEN CONSIDERED a universal human phenomenon throughout centuries. We engage in self-deception any time the truth is uncomfortable to us. As philosopher Greg Bahnsen points out, "From what was said about it by Plato, Rousseau, Goethe, Schopenhauer, and Nietzsche, one would learn how dubious a view it is that men really want the truth when the truth happens to be uncomfortable for them."[1] Concerning how we handle uncomfortable truths, Badgett notes, "Self-deception, then, is rooted in a motivational bias to protect and provide for the (supposed) wellbeing of the self by hiding (i.e., dissociating) unpleasant realities and by focusing instead on that which reinforces the convenient fiction."[2]

We commonly encounter self-deception in our lives. One example would be drug and alcohol addiction—addicts typically deceive themselves into believing they are in full control or they have no control at all.[3]

---

1. Bahnsen, "Crucial Concept of Self-Deception," 11.
2. Badgett, "Christian Self-Knowledge," 238–39.
3. Levy, "Who's Fooling Who?," 6–10.

Though these are polar opposite ways to view their addictions, both involve self-deception in their refusal to face the truth about themselves.

Existentialist philosopher Jean-Paul Sartre regarded self-deception as the primary avenue for evading self-awareness, and he called it "bad faith" to communicate a stronger overtone of blame and moral responsibility than self-deception.[4] The tendency to rationalize or reinterpret evidence is a very important hallmark of self-deception. When our cherished belief is challenged, self-deception comes into play to manipulate the evidence to defend our belief. For example, when the Pharisees heard that people were amazed at Jesus' healing power and responded by saying, "Can this be the Son of David?" they could not bear to believe that a blasphemer and a law-breaker in their eyes could be the Messiah. So they decided to believe that Jesus was healing and casting out demons by the power of Beelzebul (Matt 12:23–24; Mark 3:22; Luke 11:14–15). Beelzebul means "lord of flies" and was used to refer to Satan. Jesus replied to this by pointing out that a divided kingdom falls and that their own sons cast out demons, but his reasoning fell on deaf ears as they continued with their belief that Jesus was not the Messiah.

Philosophers have long discussed whether self-deception believes and disbelieves the same proposition. Furthermore, they have debated whether self-deception is conscious or unconscious, cognitive or volitional, intentional or unintentional, and whether it results in culpability or not. Let's address these questions.

First, does self-deception believe and disbelieve the same proposition? Raphael Demos wrote an article "Lying to Oneself" in 1960, which started a critical scrutiny of the notion of self-deception among the philosophers of the twentieth century.[5] One of the issues debated was whether self-deceivers must believe and disbelieve the same proposition, which self-deception seems to require. It sounds contradictory and paradoxical, so various non-contradictory models have been proposed. However, it is not unusual that what we believe deep in our hearts is sometimes different from what we tell ourselves we believe. A cancer patient knowing in her heart that she is dying may believe (because she wants to believe) that she is on her way to recovery. In this way, self-deception can involve believing and disbelieving the same thing—that she is going to die. Demos argues, "Self-deception exists . . . when a person lies to himself, that is to say, persuades

---

4. Botha, "Theology, Rationality and Truth-Claims," 101–2.
5. Demos, "Lying to Oneself," 588–94.

himself to believe what he *knows* is not so. In short, self-deception entails that B believes both *p* and *not-p* at the same time."[6] Demos argues that self-deceivers are responsible for their deception because they choose to believe and act their lies, while failing to act according to their true belief. When we say that self-deception involves believing and disbelieving the same thing, we need to qualify it by distinguishing between our true belief (what we truly believe deep down) and false belief (what we are telling ourselves we believe).

The second question that philosophers wrestle with is whether self-deception is conscious or unconscious. If self-deception involves believing and disbelieving the same proposition, then it raises the question of how this can be done. One common way of explaining it is to distinguish between conscious beliefs and unconscious beliefs—self-deception involves consciously believing something, while unconsciously disbelieving it. The cancer patient mentioned above consciously believes that she will live, but unconsciously disbelieves it. Jean-Paul Sartre rejected the notion of unconscious knowledge and argued that all knowing is conscious knowing because Sartre believed that all mental activity must be conscious.[7] The famous psychologist Sigmund Freud is generally acknowledged as popularizing the notion of the unconscious mental processes.[8] Freud used an iceberg model of the mind: the conscious mind is the visible tip of the iceberg, and beneath the surface is the hidden and larger unconscious realm. Today, the majority opinion of philosophers is that self-deception involves unconscious mental processes because much of our thought processes such as repressed feelings, hidden memories, habits, automatic responses, and behaviors influenced by underlying psychological processes are carried out without conscious awareness.

Another question that is often raised is whether self-deception is more volitional or cognitive. Is it a matter of our actions—focusing our attention and selecting our sources of evidence—or it is more a matter of belief and knowledge? Though some philosophers argue that self-deception primarily has to do with our beliefs and thus is cognitive, Herbert Fingarette is one of the main proponents of the volitional view of self-deception.[9] He argues that self-deception is a matter of volitional action, a disavowal, or refusal to

---

6. Demos, "Lying to Oneself," 588. Italics original.
7. Wood, "Self-Deception and Bad Faith," 211.
8. Freud, *Unconscious*.
9. Fingarette, *Self-Deception*.

spell out (make explicit) our undesirable "life engagements," and proposes that consciousness is the exercise of spelling out our engagement in the world. To put it another way, consciousness is self-awareness.[10] According to Fingarette, self-deception happens when we avoid becoming explicitly conscious of some features of our engagement in the world by disavowing our engagement; that is, refusing to acknowledge it to ourselves. It seems safe to view that most philosophers acknowledge both cognitive and volitional elements in self-deception as they are very closely associated with each other and impossible to separate.

One other question to consider is whether self-deception is intentional or unintentional. Alfred Mele is one of the best-known proponents of the unintentional view of self-deception.[11] He argues that we do not need to posit an intention in self-deception because most cases of self-deception simply involve a false belief motivated by desire. Desire, anxiety, or fear produces bias in favor of false beliefs in the face of a preponderance of counter-evidence. Self-deception is a motivated failure of self-knowledge, a false view of ourselves motivated by our desire. Many other philosophers take the more traditional approach of intentional self-deception modeled after interpersonal deception—when A deceives B, in most cases it involves an intention to deceive.[12] Though the debate continues today between intentional and unintentional models of self-deception,[13] the Bible seems to teach that self-deception is intentional, though not necessarily conscious, and it involves a choice to hold a belief about ourselves while having a veiled awareness that the belief is false.[14] Thus, according to the Scripture, self-deception is intentional at a subconscious level (since in order for self-deception to be successful, it has to be hidden from the conscious mind) and such intentionality seems to make the self-deceived culpable.

This raises the question of the culpability of self-deceivers. Philosophers continue to discuss the relationship between self-deception and responsibility. Do the self-deceivers have control over acquiring and maintaining their self-deceptive beliefs? Some view self-deceivers as victims of

---

10. Though consciousness is difficult to define, for this book I am simply defining consciousness as self-awareness.

11. Mele, *Self-Deception Unmasked*.

12. E.g., Billon, "Have We Vindicated," 6.

13. E.g., Lauria and Presismann, "What Does Emotion Teach," 70–94.

14. Though Mele rejects that intention is necessary for self-deception, his explanation of self-deception seems to require not just belief and desire but intention (cf. Nicholson, "Cognitive Bias, Intentionality," 45–58; Cerovac, "Intentionalism as a Theory," 145–50).

mental breakdown, but others object that such a view approaches self-deceivers as neurotics when the truth is that self-deception is a general human phenomenon. The majority of philosophers see self-deceivers as morally responsible in rationalizing unethical behaviors and refusing to engage in self-scrutiny especially when the consequences of their actions could involve grave harm to others.[15]

To sum up these discussions, self-deception involves unconscious mental processes,[16] has both cognitive and volitional elements, and keeps self-deceivers from conscious awareness of uncomfortable truths about themselves.[17] Much philosophical discussion of self-deception is centered on a lack of self-knowledge.[18] We are culpable for our self-deception since we are responsible for how we choose to interpret the evidence and hide the truth from ourselves.[19] We are responsible even for our ignorance because, in self-deception, ignorance is willful as we actively resist becoming more aware of ourselves before God as sinners.

Lastly, let's briefly take a look at the social dimension of self-deception. We shape our self-conceptions partially by our perceptions of what other people think of us. Therefore, we present ourselves to others in a way we would like to be perceived, and they often tell us what we want to hear, facilitating our self-deception. There is greater danger of collective self-deception than individual self-deception not only because group dynamics can aid our self-deception but also because a group has the potential to commit far greater acts of evil while deceiving themselves into believing that they are doing what is right. We hold accountable companies that practice careless aircraft maintenance because the lives of hundreds of passengers are at stake. DeWeese-Boyd calls attention to the danger of collective self-deception:

> While self-deception at an individual level may be serious enough, collectively it takes on monstrous proportions—e.g., the catastrophic ecological effects and deeply exploitive social relations

---

15. Baron, "What Is Wrong," 431–49.

16. One helpful understanding of the unconscious comes from Jung: "Everything of which I know, but of which I am not at the moment thinking; everything of which I was once conscious but have now forgotten; everything perceived by my senses, but not noted by my conscious mind" (Kam, "Overcoming Self-Deception," 139, citing Jung). This unconscious mind continues to influence our conscious minds.

17. Pak, "Self-Deception in Current," 13–21.

18. E.g., Fernández, "Self-Deception and Self-Knowledge," 379–400.

19. Kinghorn, "Spiritual Blindness, Self-Deception," 527–45.

our current consumptive patterns underwrite. Not only can such collective self-deception have calamitous consequences, it also proves much more difficult to escape.[20]

SELF-DECEPTION IN THEOLOGY

Self-deception is important not only to philosophers—it is also an important theological concept. Augustine, in his book *Confessions*, shows his awareness of his own self-deception. He says that he is not much concerned with the allurements of smells because he does not find them particularly tempting and he can easily live without them. However, he then adds that he could be deceived about this because much in his heart is hidden so he cannot trust his mind to be accurate in its inquiry into it "because that which is already in it is, for the most part, concealed, unless experience reveal [sic] it."[21]

Augustine knows that most of what is in his heart remains hidden to himself until it is revealed through life experiences. Later in his book, he also states, "I stand in great fear of my 'secret faults,' which Thine eyes perceive, though mine do not. For in other kinds of temptations I have some sort of power of examining myself; but in this, hardly any."[22] Augustine is expressing his trepidations about the possibility of his self-deception because of his inability to know his heart.

Self-deception is closely connected to sin. Just as we replace God with idols as sinners, we replace truth with falsehood as self-deceivers. The unbeliever will not believe the truth because he is a sinner and his judgment is infected by sin, but he is comfortable with his sin and does not want to see himself as a sinner. Since Augustine, theologians have viewed self-deception as a division of the will—our desire to maintain a separate, selfish will from God's will alienates us from God and reality. Since the fall when Adam and Eve rejected God's will and pursued moral autonomy, we have become highly apt to deceive ourselves when we make moral judgments. Wood explains how Blaise Pascal, an influential mathematician, logician, physicist, and theologian of the seventeenth century, understood self-deception:

> Having spontaneously imagined a false, but alluring, interpretation of his moral situation, the self-deceiver accepts that interpretation,

---

20. DeWeese-Boyd, "Collective Self-Deception," 1.
21. Augustine, *Confessions*, X, 32.
22. Augustine, *Confessions*, X, 37.

> and reinforces it both internally, with self-talk, and externally, by acting as if it were true. He does all this intentionally, by forming long-term intentions that guide his behavior even when he does not explicitly attend to them. As he continues to divert his attention from his knowledge and his reasons for acting, his attention policies become habitual, which further enables him to persist in his project of self-deception.[23]

Our fallen will distorts how we see things and how we handle evidence, convincing ourselves that we believe something we do not really believe. We also credit ourselves for good outcomes and refuse responsibility for bad ones. Theologians consider pride as the archetypal sin, and the prideful sinners love themselves with a love that should be directed to God.

At the heart of self-deception is this disordered love for self, or pride, which keeps us away from the true knowledge of ourselves. Disordered love means loving ourselves improperly by not deriving our value from its true source—God. We create a false self, not based on truth but on our distorted view of reality. The turning away from God constitutes sin, and the turning away from truth constitutes self-deception; both are motivated by our fallen, disordered love, or pride. When we love ourselves more than we love the truth, we have a motive for self-deception. We like to view ourselves as good and true, and since admitting we are sinful is painful, we distort the truth and make ourselves the standard of what is good and true. God is the ultimate good and truth, but we lie to ourselves about what is good and true because we want to maintain that we love truth and goodness even though we repeatedly turn away from both. We care about the truth just enough to pretend to love it. In this way, we turn rationalization into sound reasoning.[24]

The danger of self-deception is especially serious when it involves our assurance of salvation. One of the best-known American theologians, Jonathan Edwards, who was very influential in the Great Awakening in the eighteenth century, uses the term *hypocrites* to refer to those who claim to be born-again believers and sincere in their claims but are not born again. These hypocrites represent self-deceived false believers. Edwards's magnum opus, *Religious Affections*, is an attempt to protect against such self-deception.[25] Edwards suggests introspection, prayer, meditation, and obedience

---

23. Wood, *Blaise Pascal*, 293.

24. For a more detailed discussion on disordered love, see Wood, "Searching for the Secret Instinct."

25. Edwards, *Religious Affections*.

as means to prevent self-deception. Relying on religious experiences, such as praising and glorifying God, and feeling confident about our own conversion experience as the basis of our salvation can lead to self-deception since our deceitful hearts and Satan's delusions can produce such experiences. For Edwards, perseverance provides the best litmus test for the genuineness of our salvation.

SELF-DECEPTION IN PSYCHOLOGY

In addition to philosophy and theology, psychology can also help us better understand self-deception, especially in understanding how it involves the unconscious part of our minds.[26] Sigmund Freud argued that all of us constantly try to hide the truth from ourselves, and the persuasiveness of his view was a major factor in psychology separating from philosophy.[27] Much of psychoanalysis has to do with self-deceptions and misjudgments of the external world.[28] Experimental cognitive and social psychology has confirmed that people tend to think better of themselves and the groups they belong to than an objective assessment of the evidence would warrant.[29] The majority of college professors consider themselves above average in their teaching abilities. This may sound harmless enough, and self-deception seems to help in coping with harsh realities of life. However, "our protective deceits become destructive when they begin to serve our need to shape a world consistent with our illusions."[30] Our ability to know what we are up to and live authentically depends on our ability to avoid self-deception.[31]

According to Fingarette, consciousness is the active skill of "spelling out," or making something clear and explicit to ourselves.[32] Self-deception is a refusal to spell out the undesirable truth about ourselves. We deceive ourselves about matters in which we have a personal stake such as our wants, hopes, fears, and emotional needs.[33] Much of self-deception takes place at a subconscious level. The psychology of self-knowledge is still in the process

---

26. Lockie, "Depth Psychology and Self-Deception," 127–48.
27. Botha, "Theology, Rationality and Truth-Claims," 101.
28. Botha, "Theology, Rationality and Truth-Claims," 101.
29. Funkhouser, *Self-Deception*, 8.
30. Burrell and Hauerwas, "Self-Deception and Autobiography," 103.
31. Botha, "Theology, Rationality and Truth-Claims," 115.
32. Fingarette, *Self-Deception*, 34–43.
33. Botha, "Theology, Rationality and Truth-Claims," 116.

of development,[34] which means that the psychology of self-deception also has significant room to grow.

In recent decades, psychologists have been attempting to investigate self-deception by empirical means.[35] How could one show that there actually are cases of self-deception? What experiments could show that? One attempt to explain self-deception is to view it as cognitive illusions, or biases in judgment leading to misinterpretation of data or selective evidence-gathering.[36] People believe what they want to believe. Pursuing understanding of self-deception by empirical means would involve questions such as "What circumstances or contexts may induce self-deception? How does self-deception affect the self-image and self-esteem of persons, their motives of self-consistency and self-enhancement? What functions does self-deception have?"[37] Sturm points out that philosophers often think of self-deception as an irrational phenomenon, but in current psychological research, self-deception is not seen as necessarily irrational, but rather as an adaptive strategy, self-defense, or self-image management.[38] Some strategies of self-deception are social strategies, such as surrounding oneself with like-minded individuals to be selective in evidence-gathering.[39] Psychologists see that social aspects play an important role in self-deception.[40]

We have briefly seen how philosophers, theologians, and psychologists view self-deception, but the most important question would be "What does the Bible have to say about self-deception?" So we will now turn to some relevant passages in both the Old and New Testaments to discover what Scripture says about self-deception and how to deal with it.

---

34. Goldbert, "Psychology and Epistemology," 165–99.
35. Sturm, *Psychology's Territories*, 179; cf. Billon, "Have We Vindicated," 1–20.
36. Sturm, *Psychology's Territories*, 180.
37. Sturm, *Psychology's Territories*, 187.
38. Sturm, *Psychology's Territories*, 187.
39. Dings, "Social Strategies in Self-Deception," 21.
40. Dings, "Social Strategies in Self-Deception," 16–23.

3

Self-Deception in the Old Testament

BEFORE I START DISCUSSING self-deception in the Bible, let me briefly mention my view of the Bible. I believe that the Bible in its entirety—thirty-nine books of the Old Testament and twenty-seven in the New—is the inspired and infallible word of God. I agree with the historic Christian belief in the verbal, plenary inspiration of the Scripture, which means that every word in the original writings of the original authors of the Bible is God-breathed (2 Tim 3:16) and produced not by the authors' own interpretation but spoken from God as the authors were carried along by the Holy Spirit (2 Pet 1:20–21). This does not mean that God dictated every word to the human authors or that they made no contribution to the Bible except to simply write down what God told them to write; rather, there is dual authorship of the Bible (divine and human) in such a way that it is 100 percent word of God and 100 percent word of man. Jesus' dual nature of full deity and full humanity provides a perfect analogy to the dual authorship of the Bible. Jesus, the living Word of God, took on humanity through the incarnation and lived, taught, and empathized with us in his humanity without compromising his deity in any way. In the same way, the Holy Spirit communicated God's word to us through the agency of human authors by utilizing their thoughts, personalities, and knowledge and by guiding them to write the exact words he intended without overriding their human capabilities, authorial intents, and theological convictions.

To know Jesus accurately, we must know Jesus not only as the second person of the Trinity, the creator and the sustainer of the universe, but also as a first-century Jew who lived under Roman rule and in a Palestinian Jewish environment. Similarly, to interpret the Bible accurately, we must know it not only as the living word of God proceeding from his mouth (Matt 4:4), but also as the words of human authors who were theologians, historians, and editors in their own right. We must seek to discover the intended meaning of the human authors as closely as we possibly can by studying their historical, cultural, and literary contexts. Thus, it matters that we recognize that the Bible was written in Hebrew, Aramaic, and Greek by mostly Jewish writers writing to their audience for specific occasions and purposes in their unique temporal, socio-cultural, and geo-political settings. To ignore this would inevitably distort our interpretation of the Bible and lead to reading our prejudices, biases, and ideologies of the twenty-first century into the text. So, it is vitally important that we give due consideration to the original language, genre, and context of a text we are trying to interpret.

All English translations of the scriptural passages in this book will be in ESV (English Standard Version) unless I specifically mention otherwise. In a few cases, I use my own translation or another translation that I believe brings out the meaning of the text more clearly. When I do, I indicate it in parentheses. In most cases, I use ESV because it uses "word-to-word" translation from a textual base that is virtually identical to the original Hebrew, Aramaic, and Greek texts. Though the original writings of the original authors of the Bible have all been lost now through thousands of years of biblical history, there are more than 10,000 Old Testament manuscripts and more than 5,800 Greek New Testament manuscripts that exist today in addition to tens of thousands of biblical manuscripts in different languages such as Latin. They provide scholars with sufficient data to recover the original writings with 98 to 99 percent accuracy. The remaining 1 to 2 percent, where scholars do not have full confidence as to the original reading of the text, does not affect any of the major Christian beliefs. With this foundational premise of my approach to the Bible, let's begin examining self-deception in the Bible.

SELF-DECEPTION IN THE OLD TESTAMENT

In the Old Testament, there are not too many passages that specifically mention self-deception. However, there are clear warnings about the heart's deceitfulness because of its corruption and its rejection of the truth. Ever since the fall, the heart has been corrupted, but it does not want to accept the uncomfortable truth of its corruption, so it engages in self-deception to maintain the façade of righteousness and hide its sinfulness. In the Scripture, the heart is the center of all our thoughts, feelings, and actions, and its corruption shows that sin is not an external problem but an internal one that starts from within and flows through the body into the world.

PENTATEUCH

The first five books of the Bible are called the Pentateuch (which means five books) or Torah (which means instruction). They are also known as the Law of Moses because Moses is traditionally known as the author of these books. Today, there are many different views on the authorship and composition of these books, but I take the traditional view of the authorship of Moses along with the majority of evangelical scholars. There is evidence of editorial activities in these books. For example, the last chapter of Deuteronomy records Moses' death. Since Moses could not have written about his own death, burial, and funeral (Deut 34:5–8), a later editor must have recorded that portion. Most content of the Pentateuch probably originated from Moses, and even the later editors who added to the Pentateuch must have done so under the inspiration of the Holy Spirit since Jesus held that every word in the Scripture is God's word (Matt 4:4; 5:18; John 10:35).

Genesis 3:1–13

> Now the serpent was more crafty than any other beast of the field that the Lord God had made.
> He said to the woman, "Did God actually say, 'You shall not eat of any tree in the garden'?" ² And the woman said to the serpent, "We may eat of the fruit of the trees in the garden, ³ but God said, 'You shall not eat of the fruit of the tree that is in the midst of the garden, neither shall you touch it, lest you die.'" ⁴ But the serpent said to the woman, "You will not surely die. ⁵ For God knows that when you eat of it your eyes will be opened, and you will be like God, knowing good and evil." ⁶ So when the woman saw that the tree was good for food, and that it was a delight to the eyes, and that the tree was to be desired to make one wise, she took of its fruit and ate, and she also gave some to her husband who was with

her, and he ate. ⁷ Then the eyes of both were opened, and they knew that they were naked. And they sewed fig leaves together and made themselves loincloths.
⁸ And they heard the sound of the Lord God walking in the garden in the cool of the day, and the man and his wife hid themselves from the presence of the Lord God among the trees of the garden. ⁹ But the Lord God called to the man and said to him, "Where are you?" ¹⁰ And he said, "I heard the sound of you in the garden, and I was afraid, because I was naked, and I hid myself." ¹¹ He said, "Who told you that you were naked? Have you eaten of the tree of which I commanded you not to eat?" ¹² The man said, "The woman whom you gave to be with me, she gave me fruit of the tree, and I ate." ¹³ Then the Lord God said to the woman, "What is this that you have done?" The woman said, "The serpent deceived me, and I ate."

Genesis 3 introduces the fall of Adam and Eve through the temptation of the serpent. We are not told how the serpent spoke human language. There are also many different viewpoints about whether the creation narrative in Gen 1–2 should be interpreted as a chronological account or a literary framework that presents various aspects of creation with no indication of how long it took for the creation. Even among those who take a chronological approach, there are several views that attempt to explain the method and length of time of creation such as young earth creationism (God created the world in six literal days), progressive creationism, or old earth creationism (God created the world in six days, but each day represented an epoch of time), theistic evolutionism (God created the beginning matters and then used the evolutionary process to create the world), and gap theory (there is a gap between Gen 1:1 and 1:2, during which Satan fell and rebelled against God, causing cataclysmic warfare between the forces of Satan and God's angels resulting in the demise of the original creation, and Gen 1:2ff narrates the recreation of the world in six literal days). The consensus of Christian scholars among this diversity is that God created everything both spiritual and material at the beginning of time and out of no preexistent material (called creation *ex nihilo*). There was nothing and no one else other than God before he created the universe. This means that the serpent, Adam, Eve, and everything in the Gen 3 narrative is part of the created order, and the narrative introduces how sin entered humanity. It presupposes that the serpent was already infected by sin, and Rev 20:2 reveals that the serpent was a manifestation of the devil: "And he seized the dragon, that ancient serpent, who is the devil and Satan, and bound him for a thousand years."

The simplest definition of sin would be disobeying God's will, and both angelic beings and humans were created with free will, so the possibility of sin was inherent in creation. God, in his infinite wisdom and love, created the world through which he would bring glory to himself and benevolence to his creation. Since the possibility of sin was real since it would not be free will if angels and humans were unable to disobey God's will, it would be safe to assume that in God's perfect sovereignty and providence, he would use even sin and disobedience to bring about his perfect plan for the world. Like a judo expert who can turn the force of an opponent to his purpose, God can even use sin to accomplish his sovereign plans. Self-deception is closely related to sin, and God even uses our self-deception in his perfect plan to glorify himself and bring benevolence to the world as he reveals his love, goodness, mercy, grace, patience, kindness, faithfulness, and the rest of the divine attributes in dealing with humanity.

From the very beginning of human history, the fall of Adam and Eve brought sin to humanity, and very closely connected to sin was self-deception as it played a major role in their decision to eat the forbidden fruit. Before they ate the fruit, they had to first decide to eat the fruit in their hearts—sin begins in the heart before it is carried out into action. In the decision-making process of the very first sin in humanity, self-deception was involved as sin and self-deception are in lockstep with each other.

Let me briefly address here who was deceived. Though 1 Tim 2:14 states that Eve was deceived, not Adam, Paul says in Rom 5:12 that "sin came into the world through one man." These two verses may appear contradictory at first glance, but they are addressing different issues. In 1 Tim 2, Paul addresses the question about the role of women in the church. The passage is riddled with many difficult questions such as whether the text is dealing with husband/wife relationship or the role of women in a church setting, how much the cultural context of the city of Ephesus (Timothy was in Ephesus, a city with the temple of the goddess Artemis where women played prominent roles) should be considered in interpreting the passage, and what the meaning of the word αὐθεντέω (*authenteo*, "exercise authority") in verse 12 is where it says a woman should not exercise authority over a man. This passage is a battleground between complementarians who see different roles between men and women in church leadership and egalitarians who do not see such differences.

In Rom 5:12 Paul is dividing humanity into two groups—one in Adam and the other in Christ. Though strictly speaking, it was Eve who first sinned before Adam, Paul says that it was Adam through whom sin came into the world. Paul is treating Adam and Eve as a family and Adam as the person responsible for their decisions. The Genesis account does not tell us details about whether Adam was also deceived or not, and 3:6 simply states, "and she also gave some to her husband who was with her, and he ate." Then the text reports what happened to both as a result: "Then the eyes of both were opened..." (v. 7). Since I am not discussing the individual roles Adam and Eve played in the fall but how sin and self-deception are related, I will treat Adam and Eve as a family and not distinguish between their different responsibilities or distinct roles in the fall.

In Gen 3:13, the words "deceived me" occur in Eve's response to God when he confronts her about eating the forbidden fruit. The deception begins with the serpent's temptation in 3:1 when he asks Eve, "Did God actually say, 'You shall not eat of any tree in the garden'?" Then the serpent contradicts God's word, saying, "You will not surely die" (3:4), and adds, "For God knows that when you eat of it your eyes will be opened, and you will be like God, knowing good and evil" (3:5). This was partially true since after they ate the fruit, God said that they had become "like one of us in knowing good and evil" (3:22). Satan often uses partial truth to deceive us. He even quoted the Scriptures in trying to tempt Jesus (Matt 4:6 citing Ps 91:11–12).

There are many interpretations of the meaning of the knowledge of good and evil, but the most probable meaning seems to be wisdom.[1] Eve turned the temptation of the serpent into a quest for wisdom.[2] Nothing is wrong with pursuing wisdom, but to do so in rejection of divine revelation is to foolishly assert human autonomy and abandon the fear of the Lord which is the beginning of true knowledge (Prov 1:7).[3] If we ignore God's word, we do not know as we should know because without divine revelation, accurate knowledge of God, man, and the world is beyond human grasp. This attempt to gain wisdom apart from God is what God had forbidden for Adam and Eve because it would only bring them harm and

---

1. Wenham, *Genesis 1–15*, 63–64: "This interpretation appears to be confirmed by Ezek 28, the closest parallel to Gen 2–3, which in highly mythological language describes how the king of Tyre was expelled from Eden for overweening pride and claiming himself to be 'wise as a god' (28:6, 15–17)."

2. Sailhamer, *Genesis*, 86.

3. Wenham, *Genesis 1–15*, 63.

not good. In a sense, the tree of the knowledge of good and evil was a visual reminder to Adam and Eve that their identity, significance, and human flourishing came from trusting and obeying God, not by pursuing wisdom and self-sufficiency apart from God.

The serpent enticed them to assert their autonomy and try to make themselves "like God,"[4] and Adam and Eve succumbed to the temptation rather than trusting and obeying God's word, having been deceived into thinking that it would be good for them. Ironically, through their desire to become like God in their own way, their image of God (resemblance to God) was severely marred, though not eradicated (Jas 3:9). Choosing independence from God severed their covenant relationship of trust and love with God. After eating the forbidden fruit, Adam and Eve no longer wanted to be in God's presence and hid themselves among the trees when God called them. Having desired to become like God in their exercise of moral autonomy, they had become estranged from God.[5]

Satan's deception worked in tandem with Eve's self-deception. Satan's temptation successfully planted in Eve a wrongful desire to eat the forbidden fruit, and she deceived herself into reasoning that it was good for her to eat it (3:6a "So when the woman saw that the tree was good for food, and that it was a delight to the eyes, and that the tree was to be desired to make one wise...").[6] God had clearly warned Adam earlier that they should not eat of the tree lest they die: "And the Lord God commanded the man, saying, 'You may surely eat of every tree of the garden, but of the tree of the knowledge of good and evil you shall not eat, for in the day that you eat of it you shall surely die'" (Gen 2:16–17). But they refused to believe God's word and took delight in unrighteousness by going against God's good and perfect will for them. Not trusting God's word and desiring what God forbade caused Adam and Eve to eat the forbidden fruit. This is how sin began, and this is why the final judgment will come upon all those who follow in their footsteps (2 Thess 2:12, "in order that all may be condemned who did not believe the truth but had pleasure in unrighteousness").

Self-deception started when the first couple chose to conceive reality according to their desires rather than God's word, establishing themselves as the criterion of truth.[7] A basic tenet of self-deception is that it

---

4. Fitzmyer, *Romans*, 468.
5. Hartley, *Genesis*, 68.
6. Cf. Floyd, "How to Cure Self-Deception," 66.
7. Geske, "Solidarity in the Fall," 87.

obscures the way that we experience reality because sinful desires deceive and relativize its meaning.⁸ "Human ego deceives itself by seeking its own satisfaction; it redefines reality in order to prevent being confronted by it."⁹ When Gen 3:6 says that "the woman saw that the tree was good for food," the same Hebrew word for "good" (טוֹב, *tob*) was used in Gen 1 when God declared his created order "good" (1:4, 10, 12, 18, 25, 31). This verbal echo suggests that Eve usurped God's role in determining what is "good."¹⁰ Eve chose to define good and evil on her own terms, and as a result, she became estranged from reality.¹¹

Humans still set themselves up as the source of rationality and the criterion of all critical thought in a similar way.¹² For example, the Enlightenment emphasized the autonomy of reason as the criterion of evaluation of reality.¹³ Through self-deception, humans have established themselves as the foundation of truth. This has caused untold suffering throughout history as it brought about disagreements, quarrels, fights, and wars among different individuals, groups, and nations that operated with different versions of the truth—be it political, religious, or cultural. Convinced of the veracity of their own truths, people were willing to go to war and kill and destroy those who did not agree with their version of the truth. When God's truth, or the reality, is rejected, there can be no agreement on what is true and right.

In Eve's self-deception and her decision to eat the forbidden fruit, desire played a central role. The Hebrew verb translated as "to be desired" in 3:6a (חָמַד, *hamad*) is the same word used in the prohibition against covetousness, the tenth of the Ten Commandments (Exod 20:17a, "You shall not covet your neighbor's house").¹⁴ Desiring what God forbids begins the temptation, which leads to sin and ultimately to death (Jas 1:14–15). God forbids what he does out of his love for us because he knows and wants what is best for us. Thus, desiring what God forbids stems from the failure to trust God. James warns his readers not to be deceived by the desires that lead to sin because God only gives perfect gifts, including our regeneration,

---

8. Geske, "Solidarity in the Fall," 84.
9. Geske, "Solidarity in the Fall," 94.
10. Matthews, *Genesis 1—11:26*, 238.
11. Geske, "Solidarity in the Fall," 84.
12. Geske, "Solidarity in the Fall," 88.
13. Geske, "Solidarity in the Fall," 93.
14. Matthews, *Genesis 1—11:26*, 238.

or being born again through his word (1:16–18). We should desire what is best for us, which is also what God desires for us and gives us. God's commands stem from his love and for our good, and our desires that do not align with God's word are deceitful desires.

Paul alerts his readers that the "old self" is corrupt through deceitful desires (Eph 4:22). Our sinful desires are deceitful because we believe they are good for us when in fact they only lead to sin since they are not aligned with God's good and perfect will for us. Similarly, the author of Hebrews warns against the "deceitfulness of sin" (3:13), and Jesus mentions that it is the deceitfulness of riches and the desires for worldly things that choke out the word of God (Mark 4:19). What made Eve decide to reject God's prohibition of the forbidden fruit was her deceitful desires for it. She desired what she believed would make her wise like God, but it only made her reject God's word, the reality, and a trusting relationship with God, which ultimately led to death. She desired it because she trusted Satan and not God. Sinful desires originate from unbelief.

Along with desires, pride also played an important role in this decision to sin. Since Augustine, sin has been related to pride, and in Proverbs (e.g., 11:2), pride is viewed as the antithesis of wisdom.[15] Desiring what God forbids leads to sin and sin to death (Jas 1:14–15), and this is the course of action Adam and Eve took in their prideful desire to become like God.[16] Prophet Obadiah tells Edom, "The pride of your heart has deceived you" (1:3). As a result of pride, good and evil have been redefined in the human mind: "Good is no longer rooted in what God says enhances life but in what people think is desirable to elevate life. They distort what is good into what is evil."[17] Jesus' words "not my will but your will be done" in the Garden of Gethsemane reversed the long history of the tragic human pursuit of moral autonomy that resulted in death. Jesus, as the last Adam, became "a life-giving spirit" (1 Cor 15:45) through his perfect obedience to the Father's will, resulting in eternal life for all who believe in him.

According to Pascal, the central threat to the moral life is self-deception.[18] Moral wrongdoing is usually a product of self-deceptive moral reasoning in which a moral agent recognizes that some course of action is

---

15. Matthews, *Genesis 1—11:26*, 238.
16. Matthews, *Genesis 1—11:26*, 238.
17. Waltke, *Genesis*, 92.
18. Pascal, *Pensées*, 357.

immoral but persuades herself that it is moral after all.[19] That is what Eve did when she desired to eat the forbidden fruit and chose to consider the act of eating it good, even though God had warned Adam (and presumably Eve also) that it would kill them. She rationalized her wrong desire into a good desire. As a result of the fall, we have lost the ability to perceive the true value of moral goods and have become highly apt to deceive ourselves when we make moral judgments.[20]

This explains much of the behavior of Israel during its history from its foundation by Moses, forty years in the wilderness, and the period of judges and kings, down to the post-exilic era until its final destruction in 586 BC. Their continual rebellion against God, quick turn away from him to foreign and domestic idols, and their opposition to and persecution of God's prophets make much more sense when understood in the light of their self-perceived innocence and righteousness through self-deception. During the forty years of wandering in the wilderness, they constantly complained to Moses out of unbelief, but in their own eyes, their every complaint was justified. Even the making of their own god through Aaron, when Moses did not come down from Mount Sinai for forty days, was a reasonable choice in their eyes—it was Moses' fault, not their own: "When the people saw that Moses delayed to come down from the mountain, the people gathered themselves together to Aaron and said to him, 'Up, make us gods who shall go before us. As for this Moses, the man who brought us up out of the land of Egypt, we do not know what has become of him'" (Exod 32:1).

Deuteronomy 11:16

Deuteronomy means "second law," and its name originates from the fact that Moses gave the law the second time to the new wilderness generation after the first generation passed away without entering the promised land because of their unbelief and resulting rebellion. Trust in and obedience to God's word would have given them God's rich blessings because God loves his people and desires to give them nothing less than the best. Moses himself was not allowed to enter it (Was it partly because God wanted to give him rest and let his young successor Joshua handle the seven years of war waiting for them?) and gave his farewell sermon to the next generation,

19. Wood, "Axiology, Self-Deception," 357.
20. Wood, "Axiology, Self-Deception," 357.

who were twenty years and younger when the whole congregation of Israel grumbled against God (Num 14:29). In Deuteronomy, Moses calls them to obedience and summarizes and renews the covenant before their entrance into the promised land.

In Deut 11:16, Moses warns the Israelites against self-deception and connects it to idolatry: "Take care lest your heart be deceived, and you turn aside and serve other gods and worship them." The wider context indicates that the warning is against failing to realize that it is YHWH and no other god who will provide what they need in the land where God is taking them. There was a danger for Israel to share the naturalistic point of view of the Canaanites that forces of nature must be acknowledged and appeased in the form of Baal worship if the productivity of animal and vegetable life were to be achieved.[21] Turning to idol worship and failing to recognize that it is YHWH who provides their harvest would result in having their provisions taken away and ultimately lead to their destruction. Rejecting God means rejecting the source of all provisions and protection.

The word for "be deceived" in Deut 11:16 is פָּתָה (*patah*), and it usually means "be open" or "open-minded."[22] The warning is then against not guarding their hearts against accepting Canaanite worship. A strong warning of the consequences of being deceived in the following verse indicates that Israelites will be culpable for their choice to be deceived about who the true God is: "then the anger of the Lord will be kindled against you, and he will shut up the heavens, so that there will be no rain, and the land will yield no fruit, and you will perish quickly off the good land that the Lord is giving you" (Deut 11:17). Deception takes place in the heart, which is the seat of human emotion, intellect, and will. Our desires, beliefs, and decisions all take place in our hearts, hence guarding it against sinful desires, wrong beliefs, and evil decisions is vitally important (Prov 4:23, "Keep your heart with all vigilance, for from it flow the springs of life"). We will dwell on the importance of the heart more when we discuss Jer 17:9.

God will hold the Israelites accountable for their self-deception because it is the rejection of their self-identity as people created by YHWH to worship and serve him, not any other gods, and a failure of rational thinking that there is no other god than YHWH. Some of the Israelites

---

21. Merrill, *Deuteronomy*, 210.

22. LXX (Septuagint), which is the Greek translation of the Old Testament, has πλατυνθῇ (*platynthe*, the aorist passive form of πλατύνω, *platyno*): "be enlarged (in heart)."

who would soon enter the land of Canaan had not witnessed God's power over the Egyptian gods, his sovereignty, and his protection during the exodus (meaning "exit") from Egypt forty years ago because they had not been born yet, but they all experienced God's presence and his provisions throughout their wilderness journey. Moses wanted to give them sufficient instructions in Deuteronomy on who they were as the people of God and who they were to serve. Unfortunately, their sinful hearts would soon lead them astray from YHWH to be attracted to the Canaanite gods, and they would fail to secure proper self-knowledge as the people redeemed by God through the blood of the lamb.

W. K. Clifford wrote an article titled "The Ethics of Belief" in 1879 in which he tells the story of a shipowner whose self-deception about his ship's safety cost the sinking of the ship; it has become a classic example of self-deception:

> A shipowner was about to send to sea an emigrant-ship. He knew that she was old, and not overwell built at the first; that she had seen many seas and climes, and often had needed repairs. Doubts had been suggested to him that possibly she was not seaworthy. These doubts preyed upon his mind, and made him unhappy; he thought that perhaps he ought to have her thoroughly overhauled and refitted, even though this should put him to great expense. Before the ship sailed, however, he succeeded in overcoming these melancholy reflections. He said to himself that she had gone safely through so many voyages and weathered so many storms that it was idle to suppose she would not come safely home from this trip also. He would put his trust in Providence, which could hardly fail to protect all these unhappy families that were leaving their fatherland to seek for better times elsewhere. He would dismiss from his mind all ungenerous suspicions about the honesty of builders and contractors. In such ways he acquired a sincere and comfortable conviction that his vessel was thoroughly safe and seaworthy; he watched her departure with a light heart, and benevolent wishes for the success of the exiles in their strange new home that was to be; and he got his insurance-money when she went down in mid-ocean and told no tales.
>
> What shall we say of him? Surely this, that he was verily guilty of the death of those [people]. It is admitted that he did sincerely believe in the soundness of his ship; but the sincerity of his conviction can in no wise help him, because *he had no right to believe on such evidence as was before him*. He had acquired his belief not

> by honestly earning it in patient investigation, but by stifling his doubts. And although in the end he may have felt so sure about it that he could not think otherwise, yet inasmuch as he had knowingly and willingly worked himself into that frame of mind, he must be held responsible for it.[23]

Clifford concludes that it is morally wrong to nourish false beliefs by suppressing doubts and avoiding investigation. It is wrong, not least because false beliefs held in self-deception can have grave consequences for society.

Clifford argues that, deep in his heart, the shipowner knew that repair was long overdue. His self-deception about the safety of the ship could cost the lives of hundreds of people on board. Nonetheless, he persuaded himself to believe that just one more trip before the repair would be safe enough. His desire to save money led to the loss of many lives. According to Funkhouser, philosophers require two conditions for moral responsibility: awareness of the biases that drive one's self-deception and the ability to control these biases.[24] The shipowner knew his bias toward not wanting to spend money on repair—he intentionally repressed his doubts about the safety of the ship and the necessity of a thorough repair because of the financial burden he was unwilling to undertake. He also had the power to resist the temptation to risk people's lives. It wasn't as if he could not afford the repair; he just did not want to pay a large bill.

Similarly, the Israelites were aware that YHWH was the true God and that their attraction to the Canaanite idols was wrong. They had sufficient evidence for it if they looked for it. Among other things, God was constantly with them, providing them with daily manna and other provisions and leading them with a pillar of cloud by day and a pillar of fire by night that went before them. They should have guarded their hearts from being enticed by the Canaanite idols. In Deuteronomy 11:18–32, Moses tells the people how they can avoid self-deception and its disastrous consequences. The Israelites were to keep God's word in their hearts and souls and let it be a constant reminder and guide for them and their posterity (Deut 11:18–21):

> [18] You shall therefore lay up these words of mine in your heart and in your soul, and you shall bind them as a sign on your hand, and they shall be as frontlets between your eyes. [19] You shall teach them to your children, teach them when you are sitting in your house, and when you are walking by the way, and when you lie down, and

---

23. Clifford, "Ethics of Belief," paras. 1–2.
24. Funkhouser, *Self-Deception*, 207.

> when you rise. [20] You shall write them on the doorposts of your house and on your gates, [21] that your days and the days of your children may be multiplied in the land that the Lord swore to your fathers to give them, as long as the heavens are above the earth.

The word of God is what God prescribes as a preventative against self-deception. The word of God, the revelation of the truth about God, man, life, and all that we need to know, is what opens our eyes to the lies we tell ourselves. It brings to our awareness our biases and sinful desires and protects us against them.

Unfortunately, Moses knew that the Israelites would not pay heed to the word of God, but would go into eventual exile because of their hardened hearts that were unwilling to face the truth and relinquish their sinful desires (Deut 31:26–29). This means that even the word of God will not help us if it is met by the unbelief of a hardened heart. This is why the wilderness generation perished, and this is why God provides the indwelling of the Spirit under the new covenant to solve the problem of a hardened heart that is deceived and deceitful so it can respond to the word of God and know the truth and be delivered from self-deception, sin, and death.

In the Pentateuch, we see that sin and death entered humanity when the word of God was rejected through Satan's deception and self-deception, and what is needed to prevent self-deception is the internalization of the word of God (Deut 11:18, "lay up these words of mine in your heart and in your soul"). Through the history of Israel and the new covenant promises and their fulfillment in the church, we discover that true internalization of God's word is only possible when God's Spirit dwells in us. We need both the word of God and the Spirit of God to overcome sin and self-deception.

Jesus addressed the necessity of abiding in his word to become his true disciples and to be freed from sin by the truth (John 8:31–36). Truth will set us free from sin and self-deception. God's Spirit can use the word of God to instill the truth in our hearts. Humbly asking the Holy Spirit to help us as we daily expose ourselves to the word of God would be of utmost importance in our endeavor to overcome sin and self-deception. There is no best time of the day to do this, since people have different schedules and lifestyles; for me, the most effective way to do this is to build consistency into it so it becomes a daily routine. I wake up around 5 a.m., and I spend the first thirty minutes reading and listening to the Bible using a one-year Bible. I listen in English and try to read at the same time in Hebrew (Old Testament) and Greek (New Testament). You should find a routine that works best for you so you can secure a daily time when you expose yourself to the word of God.

POETICAL LITERATURE

In the Old Testament, five books constitute poetical literature: Job, Psalms, Proverbs, Ecclesiastes, and the Song of Solomon. These books tell stories of human struggles and experiences and offer insights and instructions on how to live wisely. They date from the time of Abraham until the end of the Old Testament. Poetical literature continues the Mosaic tradition in its warning against self-deception.

Job 15:31

The author of the book of Job is unknown, but the theme of the book is clear—it addresses the age-old question of the problem of suffering. More specifically, it raises the seeming injustice of why the righteous suffer and the wicked prosper. The plot involves Job suffering the loss of his family, wealth, and health, and his friends coming to comfort him. But when Job continues to protest his innocence, they accuse him of much evil since they are convinced that God would not have punished Job if he was guiltless. Job himself cannot understand why God allows him such suffering until God shows him that there are things that God does in the world through his sovereign, wise, and loving governance that the limited human mind simply cannot comprehend. So God wants Job to trust him even when life gets hard and Job does not understand why.

After several rounds of dialogues between Job and his friends and God breaking his silence and speaking to Job, God restores his fortune and has his friends acknowledge to Job that they were in the wrong in believing that Job must have suffered because of his sins. In restoring Job's fortune and forgiving his friends, God's goodness is revealed. Job's friends committed grave injustice to Job by making false accusations that amounted to slandering or defamation in today's legal concept. They also misrepresented God, but he was willing to forgive them as long as Job was also willing (Job 42:8; cf. Matt 18:18). Now, let's look at what the book of Job says about self-deception.

Job 15:31 states, "Let him not trust in emptiness, deceiving himself, for emptiness will be his payment." This statement is made by Eliphaz, one of Job's friends, and he was later rebuked by God along with his other friends for speaking out of ignorance. However, since anyone can arrive at partial truth through God's general revelation available to all, some of what they say is true, and Eliphaz's statement in Job 15:31 about the futility of trusting in a worthless object is one of them. Every sinner is deceived in some way. He can be deceived by Satan, who deceives the whole world, by his own heart, and through the deceitfulness of sin, which promises liberty, pleasure, and gain, only resulting in pain, ruin, and bondage. In this verse, the word שָׁוְא (shaweh), translated as "emptiness" in ESV, is used in Scriptures to denote "emptiness, nothingness, vanity, worthlessness" and refers to idols or false prophecies.[25] So Eliphaz is warning against being deceived and putting one's trust in vain things such as false gods and false wisdom, goodness, or power. In short, Job 15:31 calls self-deception the act of putting one's trust in anything other than God himself, the only source of unfailing wisdom, goodness, and power.

Job is not unaware of this self-evident truth and thus does not find Eliphaz's words helpful. His response is classic: "I have heard many such things; miserable comforters are you all" (16:2); "I also could speak as you do, if you were in my place; I could join words together against you and shake my head at you" (16:4). Job tells his friends that if the situation were reversed between them, "I could strengthen you with my mouth, and the solace of my lips would assuage your pain" (16:5). Ironically, Eliphaz, warning Job against self-deception, was himself self-deceived into believing he was helping Job. But Job saw through him and spoke the truth about the fact that Eliphaz and his friends were terrible comforters since they were not easing his pain but adding to it. Job also saw that they were afraid Job might ask them for help (6:21–23).

As the dialogue progresses and Job continues to protest his innocence, they begin to increase their condemnation and even bring up false accusations. For example, Eliphaz says in Job 22:5–7 and 9:

> ⁵ Is not your evil abundant?
>   There is no end to your iniquities.
> ⁶ For you have exacted pledges of your brothers for nothing
>   and stripped the naked of their clothing.
> ⁷ You have given no water to the weary to drink,
>   and you have withheld bread from the hungry.

---

25. Brown et al., *Hebrew and English Lexicon*, 7723.

What the Bible Says about the Dangers of Self-Deception

⁹ You have sent widows away empty,
 and the arms of the fatherless were crushed.

What makes Eliphaz create such false charges? It does not seem likely that Eliphaz was the sort of person who would slander and vilify his friend casually when we consider his initial reaction to Job's suffering: "And when they saw him from a distance, they did not recognize him. And they raised their voices and wept, and they tore their robes and sprinkled dust on their heads toward heaven. And they sat with him on the ground seven days and seven nights, and no one spoke a word to him, for they saw that his suffering was very great" (Job 2:12–13). Eliphaz empathized with Job like a deeply caring friend. How many of us can sit with a suffering friend for a whole week and just be there for him or her in complete empathy without even saying a word?

So, it seems that in Eliphaz's false accusation, we see the power of self-deception at work. He was convinced of Job's guilt as evidenced by what he perceived to be the divine retribution on Job, and when Job continued to deny his wrongdoings, Eliphaz grew more convinced of Job's guilt, his unrepentant and evil heart, and refusal to acknowledge his sins. In Eliphaz's reasoning, Job had become an evil person, which made Eliphaz question any good deeds that Job was known to have done. Seeing God's punishment of Job and his stubborn refusal to acknowledge and repent from his sins, Eliphaz seems to have concluded that Job could not have done the good deeds he was known for, and he was not a righteous person. Thus, Job's reputation must have been without basis. When Eliphaz accused Job of not helping the poor, widows, and orphans and instead abusing and oppressing them, he was probably not thinking that he was making false accusations but revealing the truth. Self-deception involves faulty reasoning: it can justify or cover up evil (as Eliphaz was accusing Job of doing) and it can also make evil good (as Eliphaz was doing to Job in slandering him but in the name of revealing the truth) (cf. Isa 5:20–21).

Job 31:33

In Job 31:33 Job declares, "if I have concealed my transgressions as others do by hiding my iniquity in my heart (אִם־כִּסִּיתִי כְאָדָם פְּשָׁעָי לִטְמוֹן בְּחֻבִּי עֲוֹנִי) . . ." Job 31 is Job's final appeal for his innocence to his condemning friends. Job claims his innocence concerning sexual sins, injustice, failure to help the needy, idolatry, and self-deception. The words translated "as others do" (בְּאָדָם, *keadam*) in this verse literally mean "like Adam." Job is most likely referring to Adam hiding from God when God looked for him after Adam and Eve ate the forbidden fruit and shifted blame to others for their transgressions.[26] The words could also refer to men in general since, just as Adam concealed his sin (Gen 3:8–12), people in general are reluctant to confess their transgressions (Ps 32:3–5; Prov 28:13; 1 John 1:8–10).[27]

What did Job mean by "hiding my iniquity in my heart"? He was probably referring to the human tendency to turn blind eyes to our flaws while seeing those of others. Our lies trap us so often that we begin to believe them. We tell them so often or live them so smoothly that we lose our grip on reality like a drug addict in denial. Our desire to believe our own lies establishes a common ground for all self-deception.[28] Sinful desire to eat the forbidden fruit caused Eve to deceive herself into believing that eating the fruit would be good for her even though God had warned that it would bring death. Sinful desires, self-deception, and sin are all very closely connected.

Job knew the evil of turning blind eyes to his sins and declares in this verse that he did not commit such sin. In Pascal's view, the unwillingness to recognize our sins constitutes self-deception: "It is no doubt an evil to be full of faults, but it is a still greater evil to be full of them and unwilling to recognize them, since this entails the further evil of deliberate self-delusion."[29] In Job 31, Job lists self-deception along with other sins such as lustful eyes (v. 1), falsehood and deceit (v. 5), failure to guard the heart (vv. 7, 9), injustice (v. 13), lack of charity (vv. 16–23), idolatry (vv. 24–27), and hatred of enemies (v. 29). For Job, self-deception is a sin just as serious as these other sins.

Proverbs 12:15

Proverbs is a compilation of wisdom sayings, a collection of practical advice based on divine perspective and the shared human experience, helping readers gain skills for living well. Proverbs 12:15 says, "The way of a fool is right in his own eyes, but a wise man is he who listens to counsel."

---

26. Clines, *Job 21–37*, 1030; Andersen, *Job*, 244.
27. Alden, *Job*, 308.
28. Funkhouser, *Self-Deception*, 67.
29. Pascal, *Pensées*, 348.

As Murphy points out, "Any conclusion that relies on 'one's own eyes' can easily be a case of self-deception."[30] In self-deception, there is a failure to assess oneself accurately or objectively: "The possibility of self-deception counts against any supposed 'scientific' objectivity respective to God and self. . . . our most sincere and discerning judgments can never be wholly trusted because self-deception distorts self-knowledge and obscures all that we think we know of ourselves."[31] In Proverbs 12:15, this failure to achieve accurate self-knowledge is connected to the failure to receive accurate feedback from others. A self-deceived fool is contrasted with a wise person who listens to counsel: "a wise man is he who listens to counsel."

Lack of accurate feedback from others can be due to various factors such as the absence of a community that can provide honest input, dishonest feedback that reinforces one's self-deception, or stubborn refusal to pay heed to other people's advice. False feedback that reinforces one's self-deception happens regularly when people are not willing to be honest with one another because of a lack of courage or a selfish desire to stay in favor while being indifferent to the well-being of the self-deceived. For example, a mother is deceiving herself about her son's habit of stealing. The neighbors all know about this, but they are not willing to tell her the truth and, instead, go along with her lies when she tells them that he is an upright and trustworthy young man. Encouraged by their acquiescence, she can strengthen her belief that he does not steal even though she has seen money disappearing from her purse when there was no one else around except her son. She carefully averts her attention from such memories whenever they come to her mind. As Dings points out, "Many researchers would agree that what other people do, say, don't do or don't say is information that a self-deceiver can treat in a motivationally biased way."[32]

An example of an extreme case of social influences on self-deception is the Stockholm Syndrome in which the victims develop positive feelings toward the kidnappers and further the agenda of the kidnappers to cope with their extreme and terrifying situation. The name of the syndrome is derived from a botched bank robbery in Stockholm, Sweden, in 1973 when four employees of Sveriges Kreditbank were held hostage in the bank's vault for six days.[33] During the standoff, a bond developed between the captives and

---

30. Murphy, *Proverbs*, 91.
31. Badgett, "Christian Self-Knowledge," 244.
32. Dings, "Social Strategies in Self-Deception," 16.
33. Lambert, "Stockholm Syndrome," para. 1.

the captors. One hostage told the Swedish prime minister during a phone call that she fully trusted her captors but feared that she would die in a police assault on the building.[34] Psychologists believe that the victim's desire to survive trumps the urge to hate the person who created the situation.[35]

The social strategies in self-deception that involve group dynamics boost our confidence that our biased perception of reality is indeed an accurate one. The more people share our false beliefs, the more confident we grow in them while suppressing our true beliefs from surfacing to consciousness. Collective self-deception involves peer pressure and greater evidence distortion as other people participate in self-deception with us. There must have been members of Nazi Germany who were deemed as decent human beings in their society and as good parents and spouses in their families, but collectively they deceived themselves into believing that they were serving humanity by eliminating certain groups of people such as Jews and gypsies.

Proverbs 12:15 tells us that there is a connection between one's self-deception and one's relationship with other people. Good relationships with wise and caring people can deter self-deception as those people speak the truth into our lives and help us see ourselves without distortion. When such a relationship that offers transparency is absent, there is little safeguard against self-deception. Choosing who we spend time with is indeed a very important decision that can either encourage or discourage our self-deception.

In addition to Prov 12:15, several other verses in Proverbs similarly warn strongly against the dangers of self-deception in self-assessment: Prov 26:5, "Answer a fool according to his folly, lest he be wise in his own eyes"; 26:12, "Do you see a man who is wise in his own eyes? There is more hope for a fool than for him"; 26:16, "The sluggard is wiser in his own eyes than seven men who can answer sensibly"; 28:11, "A rich man is wise in his own eyes, but a poor man who has understanding will find him out." These verses show that self-deception is closely related to the sin of pride, which is disordered self-love.

Commenting on 26:12, Alden remarks, "Pride or self-deception is Satan's most powerful tool. The ones who least think they need deliverance are the very ones who need it most."[36] It is the failure of self-knowledge that

---

34. Lambert, "Stockholm Syndrome," para. 1.
35. Lambert, "Stockholm Syndrome," paras. 3–4.
36. Alden, *Proverbs*, 187.

defines the fool.[37] Calvin believed that true wisdom consists almost entirely of the knowledge of God and self-knowledge, and these two are so closely tied together that it is difficult to determine which comes first.[38] All our faculties came from God, but if we do not realize our fallenness, we will not turn to God. As long as we are unknown to ourselves, we are disposed to rest in ourselves.[39] So we need some self-knowledge before we can know God. At the same time, we can never gain true self-knowledge until we have some knowledge of God and look into ourselves with that knowledge. Our innate pride causes us to see ourselves as just, upright, wise, and holy until we are convinced by clear evidence of our injustice, vileness, folly, and impurity.[40] We are all naturally prone to hypocrisy, and "any empty semblance of righteousness is quite enough to satisfy us instead of righteousness itself."[41] Because everyone around us is tainted with great impurity, as long as we keep our mind within the confines of humanity, anything that looks in some small degree less defiled delights us as if it were purest.[42] This is why the knowledge of God is necessary for accurate self-knowledge:

> So long as we do not look beyond the earth, we are quite pleased with our own righteousness, wisdom, and virtue; we address ourselves in the most flattering terms, and seem only less than demigods. But should we once begin to raise our thoughts to God . . . what formerly delighted us by its false show of righteousness will become polluted with the greatest iniquity; what strangely imposed upon us under the name of wisdom will disgust by its extreme folly.[43]

Ironically, someone who thinks he or she is wise is actually a fool who is self-deceived. Hence Paul's warning: "Let no one deceive himself. If anyone among you thinks that he is wise in this age, let him become a fool that he may become wise" (1 Cor 3:18).

---

37. Fox, *Proverbs 10–31*, 797.
38. Calvin, *Institutes* 1.1.1.
39. Calvin, *Institutes* 1.1.1.
40. Calvin, *Institutes* 1.1.2.
41. Calvin, *Institutes* 1.1.2.
42. Calvin, *Institutes* 1.1.2.
43. Calvin, *Institutes* 1.1.2.

Proverbs 14:8

Proverbs 14:8 states, "The wisdom of the prudent is to discern his way, but the folly of fools is deceiving." The wisdom of the prudent lies "not so much in cleverness and tactical talents as in self-awareness."[44] Because the first half of the verse alludes to wisdom's benefit to its possessor, the second half speaks of folly's harm to its possessor, so the deceit in question is self-deception.[45] Waltke thinks that both self-deception and other-deception may be in view here.[46] Waltke's interpretation seems reasonable since self-deception and other-deception work closely with each other. In Proverbs, self-deception is linked to folly and failure to discern one's ways, which is the opposite of wisdom. For example, 16:25 states, "There is a way that seems right to a man, but its end is the way to death."

Since the fear of the Lord is the beginning of wisdom (1:7; 9:10; cf. 15:33) and it is closely connected to shunning evil (8:13; 16:6; cf. 23:17), self-deception is then connected to not shunning evil or moral failure. Cognitive failure (e.g., inability to discern one's way) and moral failure (not resisting evil) are closely linked because the wisdom of accurate discernment comes from successfully resisting evil. It is not surprising then that many hardened criminals refuse to acknowledge their moral failures but instead blame society for their crimes.

In what way is "the folly of fools deceiving"? Fools, in contrast to the prudent who discern their way, fail to do so because they are unwilling to face the evidence. They are focused on maintaining what they want to believe is true. There seems to be a conflict in the self-deceived between true belief (what they really believe in their hearts) and false belief (what they tell themselves they believe). For example, a fool may tell himself that it won't make much difference if he slacks off a little in his farming (e.g., not tilling the land or watering the crop properly), but he knows deep in his heart that there will be a reckoning on the day of harvest. Or, a self-deceiver may tell herself that she gets by fine without exercising and a healthy diet, and she refuses to face her true belief that not taking care of her body will negatively affect her health in the long run.

---

44. Fox, *Proverbs 10–31*, 575.
45. Fox, *Proverbs 10–31*, 575.
46. Waltke, *Book of Proverbs*, 589.

There is a radical disagreement among the philosophers over what self-deceivers end up believing,[47] but according to the Scriptures, what they end up believing are their own lies and Satan's lies because they refuse to believe the truth and because they delight in unrighteousness (2 Thess 2:11–12). Proverbs 26:12 states, "Do you see a man who is wise in his own eyes? There is more hope for a fool than for him." In a similar vein, Prov 16:2 states, "All the ways of a man are pure in his own eyes, but the Lord weighs the spirit," and 30:12 states, "There are those who are clean in their own eyes but are not washed of their filth." It is self-deception to consider all of our decisions as blameless since our hearts making those decisions are fallen and will remain so until their final redemption. In Gal 6:3, Paul calls a failure of accurate self-assessment self-deception: "For if anyone thinks he is something when he is nothing, he deceives himself." We will discuss more on this verse later when we discuss self-deception in the New Testament.

In poetical literature, we see that self-deception involves faulty reasoning, a desire to believe our lies, a failure to assess ourselves accurately, and a failure to receive honest feedback. Self-deception is primarily the failure of self-awareness because of our unwillingness to face the truth about ourselves. Two things can help us mitigate self-deception: knowledge of God, which helps us to see ourselves accurately, and a community of believers who can provide wise and honest advice to us.

We cannot emphasize enough the importance of finding and belonging to a faith community not only to fight self-deception but for our overall spiritual health. The Bible makes it clear that God is a relational being existing in the community of the Trinity himself and he created us in his image, which means we are also relational beings to the core. We cannot live as God intended us to live if we try to live alone. There is no lone-ranger Christian. We are members of the body of Christ, and we need other members to function properly (1 Cor 12:14–26). Any part of the body that is not attached to the rest of the body cannot survive. Only when we belong to a community of believers can we be nourished with the spiritual nutrients we need including truth, love, and holiness provided by the Spirit through other members of the community. You must find a community of believers that will speak the truth in love into your life so you can be delivered from the dangerous effects of self-deception.

---

47. Funkhouser, *Self-Deception*, 119.

PROPHETIC LITERATURE

Prophetic literature is no exception in addressing the folly and danger of self-deception. Out of thirty-nine books in the Old Testament, seventeen of them are prophetic books, which is about 44 percent in terms of number of books. Each of them addresses various groups of people and sometimes different nations at different times in history between the eighth and the fifth century BC, but there is a unifying theme in most of them—calling God's people back to faithfulness to the Mosaic covenant promising rich rewards for compliance and dire consequences for failing to comply. In this way, they are a continuation and application of the Mosaic law provided in the Pentateuch. Prophetic messages sometimes get unpopular reputations of doom and gloom, but often their messages are God's calling his beloved people back to himself in his desire to bless them and see them flourish and not perish.

Isaiah 5:20–21

Isaiah is considered by many to be the most important prophetic book because of its many prophecies about the coming and suffering of the messiah and the eschatological restoration of the world. It is the most often quoted Old Testament book in the New Testament. Especially noteworthy is Isa 52:13—53:12, which prophesies in graphically detailed ways how the "servant" would suffer in providing substitutionary atonement for all of our sins. Though there are debates on the identity of this servant, the church has historically believed that this servant (often referred to as the Suffering Servant) is none other than Jesus. New Testament authors cite this passage as having been fulfilled in Jesus (e.g., Matt 8:17; Luke 22:37; John 12:38; 1 Pet 2:22-24; Acts 8:32-35). Isaiah is also replete with passages that tell us of great things that God will do for his people, ultimately resulting in the creation of new heaven and earth where former things of pain and suffering will be replaced by eternal joy and perfect bliss (Isa 66).

Isaiah also has repeated messages of judgment, an integral part of prophetic books, because of the persistent human failure to respond to God's good and perfect will in trust and obedience. In Isa 5:20–21, which contains the fourth and fifth of the six woes given in 5:8–23, God condemns those who pervert what is good and are self-deceived in their view of themselves:

> [20] Woe to those who call evil good
> and good evil,

> who put darkness for light
>   and light for darkness,
> who put bitter for sweet
>   and sweet for bitter!
> ²¹ Woe to those who are wise in their own eyes,
>   and shrewd in their own sight!

Distorted self-understanding ("wise in their own eyes") leads people to a distorted understanding of God. We saw earlier that Calvin made a close connection between self-knowledge and the knowledge of God. To be wise in their own eyes (v. 21; cf. Prov 26:12), people have to reject God's viewpoint (the way things truly are) and create their own version of wisdom and folly, right and wrong, and good and evil. Those who reject God's word live in self-delusion.[48] Because they reject God's revelation about himself through his word, they create their own notion of who God must be. Some hate God's sovereignty as though the exercise of it were an injustice to humans, so they decide God does not exercise his sovereignty and he lets human free will determine the future. God is reduced to a deistic God who is remote and does not get involved in human affairs. Others suppose God's love to be such that condones sin. Since God is the God of love, the argument goes, he does not condemn any sin but loves and accepts all without requiring repentance. The notion of sin is diminished or rejected. Some even deny God's existence altogether saying, "There is no God." When God's word is rejected, any random idea about God can be adopted as is the case in this postmodern world that rejects the truth God reveals in his word.

In the passage above, we can see both volitional and cognitive elements of self-deception. The cognitive element is caused by the volitional one: "who put darkness for light and light for darkness, who put bitter for sweet and sweet for bitter" (v. 20). Those who view light and darkness and sweet and bitter in opposite ways do so because they choose to. They delight in unrighteousness but at the same time want to consider themselves righteous, so they change what righteousness looks like. They redefine reality to prevent being confronted by it.[49] Because they consider their unrighteous selves as righteous in their exercise of moral autonomy and in their unwillingness to turn from their sinful desires, they consider righteousness as unrighteous and view righteous people as unrighteous sinners. As Oswalt puts it, "If the ethical imperative is dependent upon human reason alone, that

---

48. House, *Isaiah*, 153.
49. Geske, "Solidarity in the Fall," 94.

reason is no match for rampant self-interest. In fact, self-interest will press reason into service to justify its own behavior."[50] Since sinners are prone to self-deception, any empty semblance of righteousness is quite enough to satisfy them instead of true righteousness.[51] Cain may have killed Abel because, in his blinding jealousy, he came to regard Abel as evil and himself as righteous. There is no evidence that Cain repented of his sin or considered himself deserving of God's punishment (Gen 4:8–16).

Isaiah pronounces woes on those who call darkness light and evil good (Isa 5:20). Isaiah is addressing those in relentless pursuit of material wealth (vv. 8–10), those consumed by strong drinks and wanton pleasures and who consider themselves heroes and valiant men for their ability to mix and drink strong wines (vv. 11–12, 21–22), those who show no fear of God and express contempt for the slowness of his judgment in their defiant sinfulness (vv. 18–19), and wicked judges who rendered unjust verdicts condemning the innocent and acquitting the guilty (v. 23). What they all have in common is that they consider evil good, and good evil. All the while, their intention to deceive themselves is hidden from their consciousness, so in their conscious mind, their actions are good, and those who do good are viewed as wicked. Their reasoning is irrational and immoral, and they do not objectively interpret evidence because of their subconscious intention to conceal the truth from themselves. There is a tension between what they truly believe subconsciously and what they present to themselves as true to their conscious minds.

But what is this subconsciousness or unconsciousness? Even the concept of consciousness is notoriously difficult to define, and there is a lack of any agreed-upon theory of consciousness. There are many different theories that try to explain consciousness, including one that involves quantum mechanics! For the purpose of our discussion on self-deception in the Bible, and at the risk of oversimplification, I will define consciousness as present awareness. Unconsciousness then would be the lack of present awareness. According to Carl Jung, the founder of analytical psychology, the unconscious mind is "everything of which I know, but of which I am not at the moment thinking; everything of which I was once conscious but have now forgotten; everything perceived by my senses, but not noted by my conscious mind."[52] This unconscious mind continues to influence our

---

50. Oswalt, *Book of Isaiah*, 165.
51. Calvin, *Institutes* 1.1.2.
52. Kam, "Overcoming Self-Deception," 139, citing Jung.

conscious mind. Jung also believed that the unconscious is made up of a myriad of ideas and associated thoughts and feelings that function with almost an autonomous life of their own.[53] Several Christian theologians who were trained in Jung's thoughts consider the unconscious a synonym for the heart.[54] Just as the vast majority of an iceberg cannot be seen, most of our thoughts occur in the unconscious mind or our heart.

Isaiah 44:20

Isaiah 44:20 states, "He feeds on ashes; a deluded heart has led him astray, and he cannot deliver himself or say, 'Is there not a lie in my right hand?'" The verb for "delude" here is תָּלַל (*talal*), which means "deceive." ESV translates it as "delude," which has basically the same meaning as "deceive." Though some philosophers differentiate between self-delusion and self-deception, I use the words interchangeably in this book.

In Isa 44:9–20, the folly of idolatry is portrayed as a man who carves out an idol with his own hands using a piece of wood from a tree he planted and chopped down. Part of it he burns to warm himself, part to cook, and part of it he fashions into an idol and falls down and worships it (vv. 12–17). Then in verses 18–19, Isaiah says that those who engage in idolatry fail to see the utter folly of worshiping an idol they made with their own hands because they shut their eyes and hearts to see and understand the truth. In verse 20, the idolaters cannot deliver themselves from the deception because their heart has deceived (תָּלַל, *talal*) them. The self-deceivers are culpable for their self-deception because they choose to shut their eyes and refuse to understand with their hearts. The idolaters chose a delusion and became deluded.[55] They do not arrive at the insight that they have been deceived, or such insight remains repressed in the subconsciousness.[56]

Isaiah mocks idolatry as folly and finds its cause in "a deluded heart" leading the idolater astray. He cannot deliver himself from this folly and he cannot see the plain truth that the idol he just made and is holding in his hand is not God. How is it possible that a person would lock himself in a lie that he cannot deliver himself from? Isaiah says that a deluded heart is the cause. The heart is where self-deception takes place and is beyond the power

---

53. Kam, "Overcoming Self-Deception," 139.
54. Kam, "Overcoming Self-Deception," 140.
55. Motyer, *Isaiah*, 280.
56. Ridderbos, *Isaiah*, 403.

of its possessor. An idol is anyone or anything that takes the place of the one true God. It includes all religions, ideologies, philosophies, theologies, material possessions, and people that we consider or worship as the ultimate goal or value in our lives. Isaiah says that self-deception is the reason we engage in idolatry. We worship those things that are not the true God, because we deceive ourselves into believing that they are what deserve our worship.

But can we not engage in idolatry simply out of ignorance of the true God, not by self-deception? The answer Isaiah gives is no, because we are the ones who create the idol. How about those who are born into a different religion than Christianity or another environment that does not afford them a chance to hear the gospel? Paul says that people are without excuse when they reject the true God because they are suppressing the truth that is available to them (Rom 1:18). More on this later.

Isaiah was sent by God to pronounce God's judgment on the rebellious people who engaged in idolatry (Isa 65:1–7). Because of their rebellion and idolatry, God judges them with dull hearts that do not understand the truth or turn to God to be healed (Isa 6:9–10):

> [9] And he said, "Go, and say to this people:
> 'Keep on hearing, but do not understand;
> keep on seeing, but do not perceive.'
> [10] Make the heart of this people dull,
>   and their ears heavy,
>   and blind their eyes;
> lest they see with their eyes,
>   and hear with their ears,
> and understand with their hearts,
>   and turn and be healed."

Self-deception is our own fault resulting from our sin, but it is at the same time God's judgment on those who reject God and his truth (2 Thess 2:9–12). Why would God make it more difficult to understand his truth and turn to him for salvation? Yet this is a wrong question, since God is not making it more difficult for anyone to understand the truth and be saved. God is sending his judgment for the decision they already made to reject God and turn to idols. As Isa 65:2–3a states:

> [2] I spread out my hands all the day
>   to a rebellious people,
> who walk in a way that is not good,
>   following their own devices;

> ³ a people who provoke me
> to my face continually.

God is patient with sinners and eagerly waits for them to repent and turn to God. He is not quick to send his judgment on them. However, when they continue to defy God and refuse to turn from their sins, God hands them over to the consequences of their sins. Human free will and God's sovereignty work in tandem with each other. God's judgment on the rebellious people with the dullness of understanding and hardened hearts in Isa 6:9–10 is part of his sovereignty working with human free will. Isaiah similarly says about the idolaters in 44:18, "They know not, nor do they discern, for he has shut their eyes, so that they cannot see, and their hearts, so that they cannot understand." Such judgment comes on those who choose to reject YHWH, the King of Israel, who declares, "I am the first and I am the last; besides me there is no god" (Isa 44:6). People of Israel are the witnesses of the fact that there is no other God besides YHWH (v. 8). Idolatry is a willful choice to reject the only true God in favor of the gods fashioned after their likings, and it is also God's judgment on those who reject him.

When sinners harden their hearts against God, God is still sovereign. God can no more limit his sovereignty, which is part of his divine attributes, than he can limit his faithfulness to us—for he cannot deny himself (2 Tim 2:13). The Bible teaches that both God's sovereignty and human free will happen simultaneously even when we choose to sin. They are not either/or propositions.

When pharaoh refused to let Israel go, the Bible states a few times that pharaoh hardened his heart (Exod 7:13, 14, 22; 8:15, 19, 32; 9:12, 34) and a few times God did (10:1, 20, 27; 11:10; 14:8). Pharaoh was hardening his heart in his stubborn refusal to release his Hebrew slaves, and God was hardening pharaoh's heart not only to bring judgment on him and the Egyptians for how they enslaved the Israelites and caused them to suffer but also to reveal himself to the Egyptians and to his people (Exod 14:4). Pharaoh's exercise of his free will to harden his heart was working side by side with the sovereign God bringing judgment on him by hardening his heart. That they can be both/and propositions, and not either/or, is not illogical but beyond human logic and comprehension. God's Trinity (three and one at the same time), Jesus' dual nature (100 percent divine and 100 percent human in one Person), and dual authorship of the Bible (100 percent God's word and 100 percent human words simultaneously) are some other examples of God's nature and works that our limited human mind cannot fully comprehend. If our finite minds could fully comprehend God and his works, he would not be an infinite God. It is wonderful to know that our God is beyond our comprehension not only in his power, wisdom, and sovereign control of the universe, but also in his goodness, grace, mercy, faithfulness, and love that will cause us to fall to our knees for praise and worship when we enter into his presence (Rev 4:8–11).

Jeremiah 2:34–35

After the death of King Solomon in 931 BC, the nation of Israel was split into the Northern Kingdom of Israel consisting of ten tribes that rejected the reign of the descendants of David, and the Southern Kingdom of Judah consisting of two tribes, Judah and Benjamin, that were ruled by the Davidic kings. By the time of Jeremiah, the Northern Kingdom had been destroyed by the Assyrian Empire in 722 BC, and the Southern Kingdom was in danger of being conquered by the Babylonians, who were the next world empire in the ancient Near East after they completely defeated the Assyrians in 605 BC. Jeremiah's prophetic ministry spanned from the reign of Josiah (ca. 626 BC), the last godly king of the Southern Kingdom of Judah, to after the fall of Jerusalem in 586 BC by the Babylonians when Jewish people went into Babylonian exile through three deportations in 605, 597, and 586 BC.

Jeremiah was a very unpopular prophet and was considered by religious leaders as a traitor because he continued to prophesy the message they did not want to hear—Babylonian exile and Judah's need to accept it as coming from God. Many false prophets were prophesying a quick return from the exile and restoration of the kingdom of Judah under King Jehoiachin who was exiled to Babylon in 597 BC for his rebellion against the Babylonian king Nebuchadnezzar. Kings of Judah had become vassals of Nebuchadnezzar from the time of Jehoiakim, Jehoiachin's father, until the fall of Jerusalem under the last king, Zedekiah. The false prophets were prophesying to people that there would be a quick release of Jehoiachin from his imprisonment in Babylon and he would return to Jerusalem and to his throne. This was a false prophecy, and Jehoiachin was never allowed to return to Jerusalem even after he was released after thirty-seven years of imprisonment. Nonetheless, there were attempts to silence and even kill Jeremiah, and it is in such a context Jeremiah proclaimed God's message to the rebellious nation.

According to Jer 2:34–35, sinners deny their wrongdoing, protest their innocence, and convince themselves that God is not angry with them:

> ³⁴ Also on your skirts is found
>   the lifeblood of the guiltless poor;
> you did not find them breaking in.
>   Yet in spite of all these things
> ³⁵ you say, "I am innocent;
>   surely his anger has turned from me."
> Behold, I will bring you to judgment
>   for saying, "I have not sinned."

In this passage, Jeremiah is pointing out the social evils due to the corrupting influence of pagan lifestyles and because the nation was hiding their sins from their consciousness and justifying themselves. It shows that self-deception involves holding a belief against the evidence. How can one deny the evidence of blood on one's clothes? It takes a refusal to look at the evidence. The picture is one of flowing robes with bloodstains on their hems from passing by scenes of violence or committing acts of violence.[57] Craigie, Kelly, and Drinkard remark that Israel's claim of innocence here seems to be genuinely ignorant of all the evidence presented to the contrary: "The true faith had been left so far in the past, the new faith had been so warmly embraced, that the voice of conscience had died completely, and the guilty party really believed that nothing would happen."[58]

In 2:35, the self-deceiver says, "I am innocent; surely his anger has turned from me," despite the undeniable evidence—the lifeblood of the guiltless poor on his clothes (v. 34). He is aware that his evil deeds incurred God's wrath, but he is able to reason himself into concluding that God's anger has turned from him. It shows that self-deception involves faulty reasoning that distorts or dismisses the evidence. God's judgment did not come upon him immediately when he committed acts of violence, so he can conclude that what he did was justifiable and declare that he has not sinned (v. 35). Such self-justification is how self-deception often manifests itself. As 1 John 1:8a states, "if we say we have no sin, we deceive ourselves."

As I mentioned earlier, philosophers believe that there is a mismatch between underlying beliefs held subconsciously and conscious thoughts.[59] This is possible because the self-deceived repeatedly avoid having the thoughts corresponding to their subconsciously held beliefs. For example, a self-deceived wife believes deep down that her husband is unfaithful, yet

---

57. Mackay, *Jeremiah*, 167.
58. Craigie et al., *Jeremiah 1–25*, 44.
59. Funkhouser, *Self-Deception*, 178–85.

she avoids this thought. Self-deception is irrational because the thoughts of the self-deceived do not integrate with beliefs, and they lack self-knowledge concerning what they believe.[60] Successful self-deception does require carefully selected attention and interpretation of the evidence to maintain a façade of rationality.

Jeremiah 17:9

Jeremiah 17:9 is a key verse in the Old Testament on the topic of self-deception. Hence, we will discuss this verse and the deceitfulness of the heart more extensively than other passages. The word for "heart" in this verse is לֵב (leb) in Hebrew, and it is used very widely in a figurative sense for feelings, the will, the intellect, and the center of anything.[61] For example, the heart thinks in Matt 9:4 ("But Jesus, knowing their thoughts, said, 'Why do you *think* evil in your *hearts*'?"), wills in Acts 11:23 ("When he came and saw the grace of God, he was glad and exhorted them all to remain faithful to the Lord in *the purpose of their hearts*," my translation), feels in John 16:22 ("So also you have sorrow now, but I will see you again, and *your hearts will rejoice*, and no one will take your joy from you"), and is conscientious in Heb 10:22 ("let us draw near with a true heart in full assurance of faith, with our *hearts sprinkled clean from an evil conscience* and our bodies washed with pure water") (italics mine). It is the center of our mental, emotional, and moral activities.

Jeremiah 17:9 states, "The heart is deceitful above all things, and desperately sick; who can understand it?" (עָקֹב הַלֵּב מִכֹּל וְאָנֻשׁ הוּא מִי יֵדָעֶנּוּ). The Hebrew word translated "desperately sick" by ESV in this verse is אָנֻשׁ (anush), and it means "incurable wound."[62] Here it is used in metaphorical ways denoting the deep corruption of the heart. After the flood, God pronounces that "the intention of man's heart is evil from his youth" (Gen 8:21). Combined with "who can understand it?" the point seems to be that, given its utter corruption and deceitfulness, which is beyond cure, our heart is unsearchable not only to others but also to ourselves. Because the conscience itself has been corrupted and cannot discern between good and evil, many of our decisions and actions are riddled with justification and

---

60. Funkhouser, *Self-Deception*, 178–85.
61. Strong, *New Strong's Exhaustive Concordance*, H3820.
62. Brown et al., *Hebrew and English Lexicon*, 605.

rationalization and flow out of impure and evil motives though they seem innocent and righteous to our eyes.

The following verse (v. 10) indicates that even though the heart is extremely deceitful and no one can know it, God still holds us accountable for the way we manage our hearts and actions that flow from it: "I the Lord search the heart and test the mind, to give every man according to his ways, according to the fruit of his deeds." The word in parallel to "heart," translated as "mind" here, is כְּלָיוֹת (*kelayot*, "kidneys"), and it figuratively means seat of emotion and affection, as involving character.[63] The two terms "heart" and "kidney" cover the range of hidden elements in man's character and personality.[64]

In the immediately preceding verses (17:7–8), Jeremiah mentioned the blessedness and fruitfulness of a person who trusts in the Lord. Verses 9 and 10 contrast such a person with the exceeding deceitfulness of the human heart and God judging each person according to "the fruit of his deeds." So, in the context of verses 7–10, the contrast is between those who trust in the Lord and those who go in their own ways having been deceived by their hearts, and God will search and expose their hearts and judge them according to their deeds.

The word for "deceitful" (עָקֹב, *'akob*) in verse 9 comes from the same root as "Jacob," the supplanter, and in Isa 40:4, it signifies a rough place, and the unevenness of such area seems to have been viewed as deceitful and liable to cause stumbling.[65] The thought here then is that, in our inner life, we constantly try to supplant the place that should be given to the Lord, and we accord priority to other objectives than trusting and pleasing the Lord in determining our conduct, and it causes us to stumble.[66] This is because the inscrutable self-deceit of our sinful nature blinds our perceptions of good and evil. The human heart, in its corrupt and fallen state, is deceitful in its apprehension, calls evil good and good evil, and puts false colors on things (cf. Isa 5:20–21). It is unwilling to know the true nature of its deeds as John 3:20 states ("For everyone who does wicked things hates the light and does not come to the light, lest his works should be exposed").

I have an innate desire to meet my needs to be happy, fulfilled, and free from discomfort and pain because God made me to bless me, not to curse

---

63. Brown et al., *Hebrew and English Lexicon*, 3629.
64. Thompson, *Book of Jeremiah*, 422.
65. Mackay, *Jeremiah*, 516.
66. Mackay, *Jeremiah*, 516.

me, for me to flourish and not to be miserable. But because of my fallen and deceitful heart, I do not desire what is the ultimate good, that is, God, but what appeals to my fallen nature, which is selfish, proud, greedy, vengeful, lustful, envious, hateful, deceitful, ruthless, and faithless (Rom 1:28–31; Gal 5:19–21). The human heart has become deformed from its original condition created in the image of God resembling his other-centeredness, humility, generosity, mercy, holiness, truthfulness, kindness, faithfulness, goodness, and love. We still bear God's image, and we reflect it in our best moments, but it has been marred by sin, and only when Christ's redemptive work is completed will our hearts be fully restored to such a condition that fully bears the resemblance of God and reflects his glory. The good news is that God views and treats believers as already fully sanctified saints because we are in Christ (1 Cor 1:2; Eph 2:6; Col 3:3).

But for now, the fallen human heart desires what is not good but uses faulty reasoning to make it seem good to us. At the center of such faulty reasoning is selfishness. All sin is selfishness, and all selfishness is deceitful. In the eighteenth century, Bishop Joseph Butler, a theologian and a philosopher well known for his moral philosophy delivered through his sermons, argued that the self-deceived display self-knowledge failure, and the root cause of vice, including self-deception, is selfishness.[67] At its core, self-deception is blameworthy for a partiality for oneself (which Butler calls self-partiality) born out of selfishness. As Butler puts it:

> They think, and reason, and judge quite differently upon any matter relating to themselves, from what they do in cases of others where they are not interested. Hence it is one hears people exposing follies, which they themselves are eminent for; and talking with great severity against particular vices, which, if all the world be not mistaken, they themselves are notoriously guilty of.... For if it was not for that partial and fond regard to ourselves, it would certainly be no great difficulty to know our own character, what passes within the bent and bias of our mind; much less would there be any difficulty in judging rightly of our own actions.[68]

We have a selfish desire to view and present ourselves as upright and moral without wanting to give up our sinful ways, which leads to a distorted view of ourselves. In fact, when we think we are wholly right, we are

---

67. Funkhouser, *Self-Deception*, 212.
68. Butler, "Sermon X. Upon Self-Deceit," para. 2.

almost always deceived.[69] As Butler puts it, many people seem to be strangers to their own characters. But we have a moral duty to assess ourselves impartially, which is the beginning of wisdom and godliness. Failure to do so undermines our integrity and keeps us in self-deception.

Our heart deceives us by embellishing the scene, arraying things in deceptive charms. Our selfish desires sway our understanding, distorting our view of the shape and color of everything, creating an illusion. Paul says in Rom 7:11 that sin deceived him by seizing an opportunity through the commandment and killed him. Titus 3:3 adds that the deception is by passions and pleasures: "At one time we too were foolish, disobedient, deceived and enslaved by all kinds of passions and pleasures." The law that prohibits us from carrying out sinful desires ironically provokes those desires.

When we sin by yielding to our selfish desires, we deceive ourselves into thinking that it is not sin and we make justification for it. It results in a bifurcation between the truth of our sinfulness and the lie of self-righteousness. Because we do not want to deny ourselves the pleasure of fulfilling those desires, and yet at the same time want to maintain our righteousness, we create an alternative reality in which we are righteous and those desires are not sinful but good. For example, I sometimes consider myself a humble person because I do not consider myself better than others and I do not feel superior to anyone in terms of competence or righteousness. But the truth is, the fact that I consider myself a humble person is itself a clear indication that I am not a humble person.

Another example would be my love for Facebook videos. There are lots of good video clips there including recent news from a variety of credible sources and collections of cute animal videos and funny stand-up gigs among others. So I used to tell myself that watching those videos, most of which last only a few minutes, is good entertainment when I want to take a short break from my work. But the truth is, watching Facebook videos does more harm to me than good as it makes me waste my time (those few minutes add up quickly) and many of them are unhealthy in their violent or unethical content. So, when I watched those videos, I was engaging in an activity that I knew deep down was harmful to me and a waste of my time. Only in a moment of clear thinking was I able to decide to stop watching them and delete the Facebook app from my phone. I am not saying that Facebook videos are all bad for all people. I am just saying that because of my lack of self-control, they were unhelpful to me.

69. Butler, "Sermon X. Upon Self-Deceit."

Self-deception is partly caused by our love of the world, which creates a false notion that it is good when in fact it is not. There is a secret wish in us that the truth should be either as our mind imagines it or perceives it to be. So we create our own reality rather than discern the truth. In this virtual reality, we magnify our excellences, diminish our defects, create our story of an alternate reality, and bury the real story deep in our subconsciousness. Much of what people post on Facebook, Instagram, or Tiktok deviates from reality to one degree or another, as people are creating stories that present their lives in the best possible light and hiding more realistic and not nearly as impressive aspects of their day-to-day lives.

If we possessed good and honest hearts, we would search diligently for the truth, and we would be disposed to judge impartially of its evidence; and, as evidence is on the side of truth, and the truth congenial with the upright mind, it would always be embraced. Paul declares that through creation God made his existence and attributes clear, but the unrighteous suppress this truth (Rom 1:18–20). Atheism is a matter of the heart more than of the head. And idolatry, which darkens with its shadows a large portion of our world, owes its origin to the deceitfulness of the human heart. Thus only fools trust in their hearts (Prov 28:26).

Under the influence of a deceptive heart, everything appears in false colors. Not only does falsehood take on the appearance of truth, but godliness is made to appear odious. Indeed, the fallen heart hates righteousness (see Prov 29:27, "An unjust man is an abomination to the righteous, but one whose way is straight is an abomination to the wicked"). But as that which appears good cannot be hated, one art of the deceitful heart is to misrepresent the true nature of godliness and holiness. The fairest face when caricatured becomes deformed and appears evil. That is how the religious leaders were able to persecute and kill the prophets in the Old Testament times and Jesus and the apostles in the New, all in the name of religious zeal for God. Jesus warned his disciples, "They will put you out of the synagogues. Indeed, the hour is coming when whoever kills you will think he is offering service to God" (John 16:2).

The truth about the state of our fallen hearts is the most disagreeable knowledge to us. Nothing is so devastating to our pride. So, instead of facing the deceitfulness and wickedness of our hearts, we feel a strong temptation to let it lie concealed, to shut our eyes against the light, and to avoid the discomfort arising from the discovery of what is so humbling. If we saw ourselves accurately, most of us would not be able to continue our way without seeking change. Knowing ourselves accurately is not easy and often painful, but it is the beginning of true wisdom. That is why Socrates' dictum "know yourself" has been so frequently quoted.

Here is a good illustration of the state of our heart that appears to be fine to us: in a vessel filled with muddy water, and the mud settled at the bottom, we have an emblem of the human heart.[70] The mud symbolizes sinful lusts and carnal desires, so no pure water of good and holy thoughts can flow from it, but many are deceived by the appearance because sometimes their lusts are at rest and sink to the bottom. This lasts so long as they are without opportunity or incitement to sin, and it is only a matter of time before occasions arise, and worldly lusts rise so thick that their whole thoughts, words, and works are filled with impurity. A man could not bear a full sight of his own heart at once since it would drive him to utter despair. Nor is any man able to see it all at once since its deception is so subtle, its corruptions so various, and its abominations so inconceivably great, that none but an infinite capacity can grasp such immeasurable heights and depths.[71] Well, therefore, has God said, "Who, except the heart-searching God, can know it?"

Jeremiah 37:9

Jeremiah 37:9 is an example of self-deception at work: "Thus says the Lord, do not deceive yourselves, saying, 'The Chaldeans will surely go away from us,' for they will not go away." Judah knew that the Chaldeans would not go away from them, and yet deceived themselves into believing what they knew in their hearts was a lie. The Chaldeans or Babylonians were far stronger than Judah, had conquered even the very powerful Assyrian Empire, and had made Judah's kings their vassals for decades including the current king Zedekiah. In addition, Judah was engaged in idolatry and many other sins that, without repentance, expecting God to deliver them from the hands of the Babylonians would only be fooling themselves. Self-deception kicks in when believing the truth is painful.[72] For example, we can think of a mother who can't live with the belief that her child is on drugs, a husband with the belief that his wife is cheating, or a new convert with the belief that he is going to hell for lack of belief. Self-deception avoids using rational standards

---

70. Exell, "Impurity of the Heart."
71. Exell, "Impurity of the Heart."
72. Ten Elshof, *I Told Me So*, 22.

for evidence whenever it suits their purpose.[73] For the Jewish people in the days of Jeremiah, it was too painful to believe that God's judgment was coming and they would be exiled to Babylon. Though they knew Jeremiah was God's prophet, they could not believe his prophecies, so they had to make him a traitor and a Babylonian sympathizer.

As we already saw, pride plays a huge role in self-deception. Jeremiah 49:16 (and similarly Obad 1:3) mentions that pride of the heart has deceived the Edomites about their safety from the enemies. It shows that pride caused them to be misled in their assessment of their strengths and safety:

> The horror you inspire has deceived you,
>   and the pride of your heart,
> you who live in the clefts of the rock,
>   who hold the height of the hill.
> Though you make your nest as high as the eagle's,
>   I will bring you down from there,
> declares the Lord. (Jer 49:16)

Their assessment of their safety was quite different from God's, which is to say that they were way off in their assessment, and it was the pride of their heart that caused them to miss the mark. Proverbs 15:18 declares, "Pride goes before destruction, and a haughty spirit before a fall."

The false prophets in Jeremiah are good examples of those who practice self-deception out of their pride. Their confidence that Israel is a chosen nation by God with covenant promises to Abraham and his descendants (reaffirmed to Isaac and Jacob and later to David) led them to possess unrealistic optimism that God would protect Judah from the Babylonians, bring Jehoiachin back from imprisonment in Babylon, and restore Davidic dynasty, while ignoring the factors that eventually led to the downfall of the nation as Jeremiah had repeatedly forewarned.

Despite the overwhelming evidence in plain sight, they refused to believe that their nation would soon be decimated by the pagan invaders. Nebuchadnezzar had expelled Egyptian forces from Palestine and Mesopotamia undercutting Judah's reliance on Egypt, already taken thousands of exiles from Judah to Babylon through two previous deportations in 605 and 597 BC, and conquered all the surrounding nations such as Moab, Ammon, Edom, and others. In addition, Judah was engaged in such rampant idolatry that, as self-claimed prophets, they should have known that it would lead to God's judgment. Only the self-deception

---

73. Ten Elshof, *I Told Me So*, 27.

born out of their pride was what enabled them to insist on their false hopes against all clear evidence.

Micah had prophesied in the eighth century BC during the divided monarchy against Samaria, the capital of the Northern Kingdom of Israel, and against Jerusalem, the capital of the Southern Kingdom of Judah during the reigns of Jotham, Ahaz, and Hezekiah, kings of Judah. So his prophecies preceded Jeremiah's by more than a hundred years, and already Micah was warning against the same type of self-deception that false prophets and other leaders of his days were engaged in:

> [11] Its heads give judgment for a bribe;
> its priests teach for a price;
> its prophets practice divination for money;
> yet they lean on the Lord and say,
> "Is not the Lord in the midst of us?
> No disaster shall come upon us."
> [12] Therefore because of you
> Zion shall be plowed as a field;
> Jerusalem shall become a heap of ruins,
> and the mountain of the house a wooded height. (Mic 3:11–12)

Micah condemned them of injustice, violence, and iniquity in 3:1–10 also and pronounced that, because of all their sins, the destruction of Jerusalem was coming (3:12). And yet, the leaders and false prophets could convince themselves that they were safe because God was with them. The destruction of Jerusalem eventually came in 586 BC, some 150 years from the time Micah began to prophesy. The false prophets of Micah's day were right in saying that no disaster would come upon them—only in the sense that it did not come during their lifetime—but they were wrong in believing that they had God's approval on them and that no judgment was coming at all. God's judgment was simply slow in coming. Self-deception made it possible for them to believe that they had God's approval while practicing injustice, violence, iniquity, bribery, and divination.

Maybe one reason why people are engaged in self-deception is the lack of immediate retribution for their sins because of God's desire to see them come to repentance without having to send his judgment. After judging the world with the flood, God pronounced that the intention of man's heart is evil from his youth, but God would not destroy the world with a global flood but continue to sustain it with his general providence while the earth remains (Gen 8:21–22). Theologians call this common grace—God extending his grace to all human beings. This is one reason why there appears to be no noticeable difference in the lives of believers and unbelievers in terms of their quality of life. Jesus commands his disciples to love their enemies because their heavenly Father also loves his enemies the same way, making "his sun rise on the evil and on the good, and sends rain on the just and on the unjust" (Matt 5:43–45).

Such longsuffering and grace of God allowed the worst king of the Northern Kingdom of Israel, Ahab, to repent from his sins and avoid God's judgment (2 Kgs 21:25–29) even though he and his wife, Jezebel, prohibited YHWH worship and instituted Baal and Asherah worship throughout the land of Israel. It also allowed the worst king of the Southern Kingdom of Judah, Manasseh, to repent from his place of exile in Babylon as a prisoner of the Assyrian king, Esarhaddon or Ashurbanipal, and God graciously restored his reign (2 Chr 33:10–13). God's patience allowed these evil kings to repent from their sins and avoid God's judgment. But some misinterpret God's reluctance to send judgment as God's approval of them or God's failure to keep his words (2 Pet 3:4). God's patience can be accepted with gratitude and as an opportunity for repentance, or it can be interpreted as God condoning or even approving sins. It leads some people to rationalize and justify their sins, believing that God agrees with their reasoning.

The false prophets' treatment of Jeremiah is a good example of how self-deceivers call evil good and good evil. In their self-deceived self-righteous eyes, Jeremiah was an evil false prophet who was a traitor to the nation by defecting to the evil Babylonian invaders for selfish reasons. They were the courageous prophets of God calling the nation to put their trust in God no matter how formidable the Babylonian forces may be. They must have reasoned that God would provide deliverance and victory against any human enemy because of his covenant promises. It was their selective reasoning that made them conveniently ignore the evidence that was against their false belief that God would protect them. They viewed their persecution of Jeremiah and attempts to eliminate him as the righteous thing to do because, in their own eyes, they were good and he was evil.

The religious leaders' treatment of Jesus in the first century AD and their eventual murder of him in many ways resembles the dynamics between Jeremiah and the false prophets. In both cases, though deep in their hearts they knew that the one whom they were treating as evil was innocent (they could not name his sins when Jesus challenged them in John 8:46, "Which one of you convicts me of sin?"), they successfully convinced themselves into believing that he was evil and it was expedient for the nation that one man should die for the people (John 18:14). The religious leaders could not accept the notion that Jeremiah or Jesus was the true prophet of God or that Jesus was the Messiah since that would have meant that they were evil, since both Jeremiah and Jesus called the religious leaders to repentance.

In conclusion, in the Old Testament, the aspect of self-deception that seems to receive more attention than others is the close connection between self-deception and the fallenness of the human heart. With the fall came selfishness and pride, which elevated the self above God and his laws and pursued its sinful desires. Since then, humans rejected God's righteousness and truth, all the while putting on the façade of godliness and righteousness. Rational failure to reach the truth about ourselves seems to arise because of moral failure such as selfish pride or sinful desires in our hearts. Self-deception is caused by sin. That is why God holds self-deceivers responsible for their choice to suppress the truth in their pursuit of unholy desires.

What can we do about our fallen heart that is filled with selfish pride and sinful desires? If you are a regenerated (born-again) believer in Christ, the new covenant promises of the Bible have been partially fulfilled in you already. You have the Spirit of God dwelling in you transforming you into the likeness of Jesus Christ, having redeemed you from the penalty of sin through Jesus' substitutionary death on the cross and delivering you from the power of sin by the powerful work of the Holy Spirit. This gradual and persistent work of sanctification (making you holy) will continue until it is completed either when you die or when Jesus returns, whichever comes first.

Though we have the Spirit of Christ, we also have the fallen nature while we are living in these present bodies, which Paul describes this way: "But if Christ is in you, although the body is dead because of sin, the Spirit is life because of righteousness" (Rom 8:10). The resurrection and transformation of our sinful body is promised ("he who raised Christ Jesus from the dead will also give life to your mortal bodies through his Spirit who dwells in you," Rom 8:11b), but it is a lifetime process. We should be encouraged since we fight from victory, not for victory, but the fight is a real one requiring our diligent vigilance in learning what is in our hearts, including our hidden motivations, fears, and desires. Daily spending time in confessing our sins in prayer would allow the Spirit to reveal our sins lurking in the recesses of our hearts.

4

Self-Deception in the New Testament

IN THE NEW TESTAMENT, there are more specific references to self-deception than in the Old Testament. Many other New Testament passages address the concept, though the word *self-deception* is not used. Like the Old Testament, a corrupt heart is the core issue that causes sin. Mark 7:20–23 states, "And he said, 'What comes out of a person is what defiles him. For from within, out of the heart of man, come evil thoughts, sexual immorality, theft, murder, adultery, coveting, wickedness, deceit, sensuality, envy, slander, pride, foolishness. All these evil things come from within, and they defile a person'" (similarly in Matt 15:18–20). In Luke 8:15, the good soil represents "an honest and good heart" that bears fruit when hearing the word of God while a hardened heart (a path), a shallow heart (rocky soil), and a preoccupied heart (thorny bushes) fail to bear fruit.

Self-deception is often addressed in the New Testament in conjunction with one's professed religion and self-assessment of being righteous or wise. I will use the term *false believers* to refer to those who are self-deceived about their religion. Paul speaks of the dangers he experienced from ψευδαδέλφοι (*pseudadelphoi*), which means "false brothers" (2 Cor 11:26; Gal 2:4). The existence of false brothers in his churches is a problem Paul addresses in many of his letters. He often warns against the self-deception of the unrighteous in regard to inheriting the kingdom of God (1 Cor 6:9–10; Gal 5:19–21; Eph 5:5–6). Those who do not have the Spirit do not belong to Christ (Rom 8:9–11) even if they are in the church. He tells the Thessalonian believers that his confidence in God's election of them comes not just from their profession of faith but from the evidence of the work of the Holy Spirit in them (1 Thess 1:4–5a, "For we know, brothers loved by God, that he has chosen you, because our gospel came to you not only in word, but also in power and in the Holy Spirit and with full conviction"). The implication seems to be that without such evidence of the work of the Holy Spirit in a person, a profession of faith in Christ may be without God's election (1:4b: "he has chosen you") that results in regeneration (being born again). Paul warns the Corinthian believers that those who yield to the same temptations of the exodus generation will also experience the same fate of destruction (1 Cor 10:6–13). Because of the false apostles and deceitful workmen disguising themselves as apostles of Christ (2 Cor 11:13), Paul tells the Corinthians to examine themselves to see if they are in the faith—if they are, then they will realize that Christ is in them (2 Cor 13:5).

Paul is deeply concerned for the Galatian believers because of the false gospel they are exposed to (Gal 1:6–9), and he is fearful that his labor for them might be in vain (4:11). So he warns them that those who engage in the works of the flesh will not inherit the kingdom of God (5:19–21). Paul cautions the Philippian believers against many professed believers who live as enemies of Christ and whose ends are destruction (Phil 3:18–19); the Colossians against self-made religion (Col 2:23); and Timothy against false teachers (1 Tim 1:3–7; 6:3–5), apostasy through deceitful spirits (4:1–3), and those who are disqualified regarding the faith (2 Tim 3:1–9).

General Epistles (non-Pauline letters in the New Testament) describe false believers in many ways that provide insights into their characteristics: false believers think they are religious but do not bridle their tongues, deceiving their hearts (Jas 1:26). They say they have faith but because they do not have works, their "faith" is dead (2:17) and cannot save them (2:14). They may have orthodox belief subscribing to correct doctrines, but demons also have the same belief with much stronger conviction (2:19). They may have bitter jealousy and selfish ambition in their hearts because they have the wisdom that is earthly, unspiritual, and demonic (3:15–16). After having escaped the defilements of the world through the knowledge of Christ, they get entangled in them again, their last state becoming worse than the first (2 Pet 2:20). They say they have fellowship with God while they walk in darkness (1 John 1:6). Even though they say they are in the light, they are still in darkness hating other believers (2:9).

John describes them as antichrists (2:18), and they may leave the believing community of orthodox faith because they never really belonged to it in the first place (2:19). They continue in their sinful life because they have neither seen nor known God (3:6). The Christ they believe is not the true Christ but a different one—for example, a christ who may be divine but not human (1 John 4:2–3; 2 John 7–9).

For all unregenerate people including both false believers and unbelievers, self-deception involves the discrepancy between their view of themselves and the truth. It takes the light of the biblical truth and the Spirit's work of revealing it to them in order for them to come to face the truth about themselves. Only then can they begin their journey toward freedom from self-deception and wholeness of being with the unity between the conscious and unconscious, and between self-perception and reality.[1] The final arrival at this will only be at the eschatological judgment (1 Cor 4:5, "Therefore do not pronounce judgment before the time, before the Lord comes, who will bring to light the things now hidden in darkness and will disclose the purposes of the heart. Then each one will receive his commendation from God"). Until then, even regenerated people indwelt by the Holy Spirit are not completely free from self-deception because perfect self-knowledge can only be achieved on the day the Lord returns and they become free from sin (see 1 John 3:2b, "but we know that when he appears we shall be like him, because we shall see him as he is"; 1 Cor 13:12, "For now we see in a mirror dimly, but then face to face. Now I know in part; then I shall know fully, even as I have been fully known"). We should think critically about ourselves through meditation on the Holy Scriptures so we can recognize that self-deception is a structural part of a universe fallen into sin until the final redemption.[2]

When the Lord returns, there will not be any more chance for the unbelievers and false believers to benefit from Christ's redemptive work of atonement and enter into eternal life. The church must do everything it can to help them out of their self-deception so they may know the truth that will set them free from sin and deception (John 8:31). It would be tragic for those who consider themselves believers in Jesus Christ to find out on the day that the Lord returns that they do not know the real Jesus and end up in eternal judgment. Satan will do everything in his power to keep them in self-deception, so helping false believers out of self-deception

1. Cf. Via, *Self-Deception and Wholeness*.
2. Geske, "Solidarity in the Fall," 97.

involves recognizing Satan's deception and how it is working with their self-deception. We must realize that the mission field is not only in remote places where missionaries must be sent to reach the lost but also in our own congregations where we have so many opportunities to help those who are tragically self-deceived about their faith. It begins with an awareness and a wise strategy to reach them with the gospel truth through the power of the Holy Spirit and through the loving community that can speak the truth in love to them.

I have grouped the relevant passages in the New Testament into three sections: Gospels and Acts, Pauline Epistles, and Hebrews and General Epistles. We will discuss them in turn.

GOSPELS AND ACTS

Matthew 7:21–23

Strictly speaking, the Gospel of Matthew is anonymous since the author is not mentioned in the Gospel, but it was universally received shortly after it was first written because the author was known as Matthew or Levi, one of the twelve disciples of Jesus. The dating of the Gospel typically ranges from AD 60s to 80s, but most evangelical scholars date it in the 60s before the fall of Jerusalem in AD 70. Matthew's Gospel is commonly known to have targeted Jewish readers to demonstrate to them that Jesus is indeed the Messiah that the Hebrew Scriptures prophesied about. There are many fulfillment formulas in Matthew in which he mentions that a specific Old Testament prophecy was fulfilled by Jesus (e.g., 1:22–23; 2:6, 15, 16, 23; 4:15–16; 8:17; 12:17–21; 13:14, 35; 21:4; 27:9–10). Matthew also had other goals, and one of them was to address the issue of the presence of false believers in the church.

In the introduction to his highly acclaimed commentary on the Gospel of Matthew, Robert Gundry begins his "Theology of Matthew" section by discussing Matthew's "great concern over the problem of a mixed church"[3] and ends the section by focusing on the mixed nature of the church: "The church has grown large through the influx of converts from all nations (28:18–20). But these converts include false as well as true disciples (13:24–30, 36–43, 47–50; 22:11–14; 25:1–13). The distinction between them is coming to light through persecution of the church

3. Gundry, *Matthew*, 5.

(5:10–12)."[4] The parable of the wedding feast mentions a guest who has no wedding garment, is without an excuse when asked how he could get in without a wedding garment, and consequently is thrown out into the outer darkness (Matt 22:1–14). This parable suggests that those who respond to the invitation of the gospel are to be composed of both genuine believers and false believers.[5] Jesus ends the parable by saying, "For many are called, but few are chosen" (v. 14), meaning that not everyone who responds to the gospel invitation has a saving faith that leads to salvation.

In the parable of the ten virgins, both foolish and wise virgins wait for the coming of the bridegroom, but only the wise virgins are allowed into the marriage feast because the foolish virgins did not have the proper preparations (Matt 25:1–13). The parable portrays the church waiting for the second coming of Christ (v. 13), so the foolish virgins appear to portray the false disciples of Jesus,[6] and the wise virgins genuine disciples. Other scholars share Gundry's view on the mixed nature of the church in Matthew's Gospel. Ridderbos sees the foolish virgins as representing people "who only pretend to watch for the Lord."[7] Greene views the parable as referring to those who may make a profession of faith and join the church but do not have the Holy Spirit.[8] In the contrast between "the wise" and "the foolish," Gundry sees Matthew's special designations for nonmembers and members of the kingdom.[9] This can be seen by the response of the bridegroom in verse 12 to the request of the five foolish virgins to open the door for them: "Truly I say to you, I do not know you." These parables support Gundry's claim that Matthew is concerned about the problem of a mixed church of genuine and false believers.

In Matt 7:21–23, Jesus warns:

> Not everyone who says to Me, "Lord, Lord," will enter the kingdom of heaven, but he who does the will of My Father who is in heaven will enter. Many will say to Me on that day, "Lord, Lord, did we not prophesy in Your name, and in Your name cast out

---

4. Gundry, *Matthew*, 5–6.

5. Gundry points out that Matthew is warning against false discipleship in 22:11–14 (*Matthew*, 439).

6. The point of the parable seems to be that "it is not enough to be 'in on the act,' to be a professing disciple" (France, *Matthew*, 352).

7. Ridderbos, *Matthew*, 456.

8. Greene, *Gospel according to Matthew*, 8.

9. Gundry, *Matthew*, 499.

demons, and in Your name perform many miracles?" And then I will declare to them, "I never knew you; depart from Me, you who practice lawlessness."

Matthew 7:15–20 deals with false prophets (v. 15), but verses 21–23 include all false believers, variously called by scholars as "false followers," "professing Christians," or "superficial disciples." Carson calls them false followers.[10] Green believes the passage is about professing Christians whose Christianity is bogus and worthless.[11] France thinks this passage is about superficial disciples who make spurious profession of discipleship.[12] Jesus' warning is issued to those who call him Lord, and their cry of "Lord, Lord"[13] reflects fervency.[14] So France believes that they are sincere, but self-deceived.[15]

Their protest that they prophesied, drove out demons, and performed many miracles in his name serves to intensify the warning that even spiritually impressive activities do not help them into the kingdom of heaven when they do not do the will of God. Three times these false professors use the phrase "in your name"—each time before "prophesied," "expelled demons," and "did many mighty works." Thus, "in your name" is strongly emphasized. Also, the fact that they are protesting Jesus' decision not to let them into his kingdom suggests that their profession of faith in Jesus is not a pretentious verbal profession but rather a sincere one. In other words, they seem to consider themselves genuine believers.

Unbelievers will not make such a claim. Nor is it very likely that false prophets and false believers who have consciously rejected Jesus and only pretended to believe in him will dare make such a claim on the day of judgment when they will know that they cannot hide their thoughts and motives from God. The people most likely to make such a claim are those who think that legitimate grounds for their claim exist—false believers who are deceived about the genuineness of their faith. The alarming aspect of this is that there will be "many" who will make such a claim "on that day," or on the day of the final judgment (v. 22). Jesus says that they will be rejected despite their profession of faith and impressive religious activities because

10. Carson, *Matthew*, 192.
11. Green, *Message of Matthew*, 109.
12. France, *Matthew*, 148.
13. This repeated formula appears only in this passage and in the Lukan parallel (Luke 6:46) and in Matt 25:11, where it also appears in connection with eschatological judgment.
14. Carson, *Matthew*, 192.
15. France, *Matthew*, 148.

they are without the inward reality of a personal relationship with Jesus ("I never knew you") and righteous conduct ("you workers of lawlessness")—they are false believers (v. 23).

True believers and self-deceived false believers look very much alike on the surface, like two buildings whose foundations are not visible (Matt 7:24–27). On the surface, they may both look very sincere in their faith and active in religious activities. Thus, Jesus' warning about those who will not be allowed entrance into the kingdom of heaven on the day of judgment takes on an immediate and urgent relevancy.[16] We are not to complacently read these warnings in Matthew's Gospel as if they are addressed to the outsiders of the believing community since these warnings are issued to those who are insiders—to those who regard themselves as believers.[17] As Ridderbos states, "His warnings . . . are loving admonitions to His disciples to examine themselves to see whether they have the fruits of faith, or most basically, whether they have faith itself. He admonishes them not to deceive themselves in their relationship to Him."[18]

Matthew 7:21–23 teaches us that false believers can make a sincere profession of faith just like genuine believers. This should serve as an alarm to all believers and to the leaders in the church that many church members, even active ones, may be self-deceived false believers who are still in need of a personal relationship with Jesus Christ. Every believer is responsible for examining her own faith (2 Cor 13:5) and should not judge someone else's salvation, which can be a risky business since it is impossible to know other people's hearts, let alone one's own as we have already seen. It is a different story for church leaders because as the shepherds placed in charge of their flocks by the chief Shepherd (1 Pet 5:4), they are responsible for knowing the spiritual condition of their flocks, and they should endeavor to make sure that not a single lamb under their pastoral care will be lost.

Luke 8:11–15

Luke may be the only gentile author of the New Testament (Col 4:10–14). Luke emphasizes that Jesus is the Savior of all people including the Jews and the gentiles, and Luke 19:10 is considered by many to be the key verse of the Gospel of Luke: "For the Son of Man came to seek and to save the

---

16. Ridderbos, *Matthew*, 157.
17. Ridderbos, *Matthew*, 157.
18. Ridderbos, *Matthew*, 157.

lost." Luke also champions the causes of the socially disadvantaged of his days such as women, the poor, lepers, Samaritans, and tax collectors. Luke wrote the Gospel of Luke and the Acts of the Apostles (the titles are not from Luke) as a two-volume work in the AD 60s. It is dedicated to a certain Theophilus in the prologue (Luke 1:1–4; Acts 1:1), who was apparently Luke's patron who financed Luke's research and writing project. Luke had other readers in mind also, and most scholars believe that Luke tried to reach the gentile readers by writing a historically accurate and convincing account of Jesus. There is a consensus among scholars that Luke was a reliable historian. Luke was a physician (Col 4:14) and a close companion of the apostle Paul (2 Tim 4:11; Phlm 24; so-called "we" passages in Acts where Luke includes himself in the travel narratives in Acts 16:10–17; 20:5–15; 21:1–18; 27:1—28:16).

In Luke 8:9–15, Jesus tells one of the best-known parables in the Gospels and one that appears in all three Synoptic Gospels—the parable of the sower, in which a farmer sows his seeds which fall on four different kinds of soil such as path, rocky soil, thorny bushes, and good soil. After telling the parable, when the disciples come to him privately and ask him the meaning of the parable, Jesus explains it for them in verses 11–15:

> Now the parable is this: The seed is the word of God. [12] The ones along the path are those who have heard; then the devil comes and takes away the word from their hearts, so that they may not believe and be saved. [13] And the ones on the rock are those who, when they hear the word, receive it with joy. But these have no root; they believe for a while, and in time of testing fall away. [14] And as for what fell among the thorns, they are those who hear, but as they go on their way they are choked by the cares and riches and pleasures of life, and their fruit does not mature. [15] As for that in the good soil, they are those who, hearing the word, hold it fast in an honest and good heart, and bear fruit with patience.

Jesus explains that the first soil (the path) symbolizes those who hear the word of God but the devil takes it away from their hearts "so that they may not believe and be saved" (v. 12). The last soil is the good soil symbolizing "an honest and good heart" that bears fruit with patience (v. 15). This fruitfulness accompanies salvation since the last soil is a clear contrast to the first soil that represents those who are not saved (v. 12). The question is the second and third soils (the rock and the thorns). Are they saved or not? Some people think they are because those represented by the second soil "believe" at least for a while (v. 13) in contrast to those who do not believe and are not saved (v. 12)—they are genuine believers who do not persevere.[19] Dillow argues that since there was germination and growth (8:6 states that "it grew up"), there must be some root in a plant that later withers and dies, symbolizing a dead and carnal Christian.[20] For Dillow, "It is possible for a truly born-again person to fall away from the faith and cease believing" without losing salvation.[21] However, not every mention of "believe" in the Bible refers to genuine saving faith. For example, in John 2:23–25, 8:30–59, and Acts 8:9–24, as we will see shortly, those who are said to have believed are not genuine believers with saving faith. Dillow's differentiation between having root and growth as denoting salvation and bearing fruit as denoting maturity is difficult to substantiate because in the parable, as in the Gospels in general, fruit-bearing is primarily a sign of salvation.

John the Baptist warned that every tree that does not produce good fruit will be cut down and thrown into the fire, which symbolizes the wrath to come or the eschatological judgment (Luke 3:7–9). In Luke 6:43–45, fruit is the determining factor between a good tree and a bad tree: "each tree is known by its own fruit" (v. 44a). In the wider context, those who do not bear good fruit are also identified as the hearers of the word only and builders on the ground without a foundation (vv. 46–49). They are those who prove their profession of faith to be without reality when trials come to their lives to test their faith. Though speech reveals the heart (v. 45b), Jesus points out the inconsistency of mere profession without substance. In Luke, fruit is the ultimate criterion by which a tree or a crop is measured (also Luke 13:6–9). It separates the good from the bad and genuine believers from mere professors.

Where is self-deception in all of this? I believe the second and third soils in the parable of the sower represent those who are the hearers of the word only, and in the end, even what they think that they have will be taken away. Therefore, Jesus warns, "Take care then how you hear, for to the one who has, more will be given, and from the one who has not, even what he thinks he has will be taken away" (Luke 8:18). They are self-deceived false believers who think they have faith. The rest of the New Testament supports the view that hearers of the word only are self-deceived false believers (e.g.,

19. Dillow, *Reign of the Servant Kings*, 399.
20. Dillow, *Reign of the Servant Kings*, 398.
21. Dillow, *Reign of the Servant Kings*, 199.

Matt 7:26–27; Luke 6:49; Jas 1:22, 23, 25). The New Testament employs several different methods including warnings and exhortations to bring them to genuine faith and salvation. God does not wish anyone to perish but all to reach repentance (2 Pet 3:9). As long as false believers remain in the church, there always remains a chance for salvation.

However, so far as they remain hearers only, there is no salvation. In explaining the parable of the sower, Jesus mentions that the secrets of the kingdom of God have been given to the disciples, but not to outsiders (Luke 8:10; Matt 13:11; Mark 4:11). Jesus is saying that it is those who have understanding by divine enablement who will bear fruit from the planting of the word in their hearts. Hearers only are those who only have superficial understanding of the word without true understanding that results in salvation. Their faith is not unbelief, which is what the first soil represents, but it is also not fruit-bearing genuine faith that the fourth soil represents. Church leaders must consider it an important task of their ministry to help these self-deceived hearers who think they believe to become genuine believers and the doers of the word.

A question may arise: If God has to give the secrets of the kingdom for anyone to be able to understand and believe the word of God, doesn't salvation depend entirely on God and there is nothing humans can do? The answer is yes and no. Yes, salvation depends entirely on God since apart from God's grace, no one can be saved. No, we are saved by grace through faith (Eph 2:8–9), and Jesus does not cast out anyone who comes to him (John 6:35). It is beyond human comprehension how God works out his sovereign plan of election that he had in place before the foundation of the world (Eph 1:4–5), but there is human responsibility to choose to believe and profess faith (Rom 10:9–10), and everyone who believes in Jesus and calls on his name will be saved (v. 13). In Matt 13:14–15, Jesus cites Isa 6:9 and interprets it to explain that those who hear but never truly understand the word of God are the ones who harden their hearts and close their eyes so they do not turn to God to be healed. Matthew contrasts them with the disciples to whom the secrets of the kingdom of heaven are given so they hear and understand (vv. 11, 23).

Some who harden their hearts are those who do not believe, and they are represented by the first soil (the hardened path) as the word of God has no place in their hearts (Luke 8:12). Others who harden their hearts are the second soil (the rocky soil) representing those who receive the word even with joy but in a superficial way, and in a time of temptation or testing they fall away because they have no root (v. 13), or the third soil (the soil covered by thorns) representing those whose cares and pleasures of life choke the word out and do not bear fruit to maturity (v. 14). These first three types of people, who for various reasons fail to bear fruit, are contrasted to those represented by the good soil, and Luke describes the good soil this way: "these are those who have good and worthy heart and, hearing the word, hold it fast and bear fruit in patience" (v. 15, translation mine). Luke makes two things determinative factors for bearing fruit: good heart and perseverance. For Luke, like the rest of the Bible, the heart is the key issue that determines one's reception or rejection of God's word and leads to either salvation or damnation. Since the first three soils are contrasted to the last soil, the implication is that the heart is not right in these three soils.

Matthew says that the good soil represents those who hear the word and understand it (Matt 13:23), and Mark says that they are those who hear the word and accept it (Mark 4:20). But Luke strongly emphasizes the good heart by using two similar words to describe it: καλός (kalos) and ἀγαθός (agathos). These words can be considered synonyms since both words basically mean "good," though I translated them as "good and worthy" since "good and good" would be a bad translation, and ἀγαθός (agathos) does have the meaning of "worthy." The primary reason Luke uses both words here seems to be for emphasis by repetition. Luke wants to strongly emphasize that it is a good heart that holds fast to the word of God and bears fruit in patience. The heart is the central factor that determines the fruit-bearing. Combining observations from the Synoptic Gospels' accounts of the good soil, we can conclude that it represents those with a good heart who hold fast to the word of God with patience when they hear it (Luke 8:15), and it leads to their understanding (Matt 13:23) and acceptance of the word (Mark 4:20) that results in the fruit-bearing of salvation.

Church leaders have a solemn responsibility to help their congregations not to remain mere hearers of the word who think that they believe but actually don't. They should teach them to hold fast to the word and persevere in it, overcoming trials of life, temptations of riches, and pleasures in the world. It will require faithful preaching and teaching of the word of God, relying on the Spirit, and living out the preaching in their daily lives so people can learn from their examples how to hold fast to the word of God when tested by trials and temptations of life. According to the parable of the sower, their salvation depends on not just hearing the word of God but then steadfastly holding on to it.

When the word of God is sown in the hearts of the hearers, before it can bear the fruit of salvation, it must first overcome the testing and temptations that come from the world. Their hearts have to become good soils that bear the fruit of salvation. Though salvation is by God's grace and does not depend on a good heart or human efforts to overcome temptations, these are the outworkings or the fruit of God's work in our hearts. Any thought that we are saved only by hearing the word even though we fall away when our faith is tested or are consumed by worldly pursuits and desires would be self-deception. Hear Jesus' warning again: "Take care then how you hear, for to the one who has, more will be given, and from the one who has not, even what he thinks that he has will be taken away" (Luke 8:18).

Luke 18:9–14

One of Luke's favorite themes in his Gospel is that of reversal of fortune. In Mary's song of praise, called the Magnificat ("magnify") because it is the first word in her song in the Latin translation (Luke 1:46–55), Mary sings, "he has brought down the mighty from their thrones and exalted those of humble estate; he has filled the hungry with good things, and the rich he has sent away empty" (vv. 52–53). In the parable of the rich man and Lazarus, we find another such reversal of fortune (Luke 16:19–31): the rich man who has lived his life in sumptuous feasting ends up in Hades (the abode of the unbelieving dead waiting for the final judgment day) where he lives in pain and remorse, and Lazarus, who lived in hunger and physical illnesses, ends up in Abraham's bosom.

In Luke 18:9–14 Jesus tells another story of reversal in the parable of the Pharisee and the tax collector:

> [9] He also told this parable to some who trusted in themselves that they were righteous, and treated others with contempt: [10] "Two men went up into the temple to pray, one a Pharisee and the other a tax collector. [11] The Pharisee, standing by himself, prayed thus: 'God, I thank you that I am not like other men, extortioners, unjust, adulterers, or even like this tax collector. [12] I fast twice a week; I give tithes of all that I get.' [13] But the tax collector, standing far off, would not even lift up his eyes to heaven, but beat his breast, saying, 'God, be merciful to me, a sinner!' [14] I tell you, this man went down to his house justified, rather than the other. For everyone who exalts himself will be humbled, but the one who humbles himself will be exalted."

Luke comments that Jesus told this parable to those who were self-righteous and treated others with contempt (v. 9). In the parable, the Pharisee thanks God in prayer for his righteousness (vv. 11b–12). But the tax collector is deeply aware of his sinfulness, and he is the one who goes down to his house justified, not the Pharisee who felt righteous because he compared himself to those who he thought were worse sinners than himself (v. 14). This is a good example of self-deception, and Jesus' parable is a warning against self-righteous people who deceive themselves into believing they are righteous before God because they are more righteous than others whom they view as sinners. Such thinking involves a logical fallacy since even if it is granted that they may be more righteous than some other people, it does not make them righteous before God. In God's eyes, all human righteous acts appear as "filthy rags" (Isa 64:6 NIV). Comparing ourselves with others will not help us gain accurate self-knowledge because it enables a self-deceived view of ourselves, causing us to believe we are better than we actually are. As Calvin puts it, we are easily satisfied with an empty semblance of righteousness.[22] The humble tax collector was the one who was vindicated before God (18:14) because he was not self-deceived about his standing before God as a sinner in need of God's mercy (18:13) and because God opposes the proud but gives grace to the humble (Jas 4:6). In this life, people are often evaluated based on the outward appearances and how they present themselves to the world, but on the judgment day, hearts will be evaluated and appearances will be reversed.[23] As Jesus said, many who are first will be last and the last first (Matt 19:30; 20:16; Mark 10:31; Luke 13:30). Luke's theme of the reversal of fortune is closely related to the biblical theme of self-deception.

Jesus uses the word *hypocrites* to describe those who consider themselves righteous and have the appearance of godliness in the eyes of people but are unrighteous in God's eyes. Hypocrites in the Gospels are then good examples of self-deception, and the Pharisee in this parable fits the bill perfectly. In Luke 13:10–17, we see Jesus calling the ruler of the synagogue a hypocrite because he was indignant that on the Sabbath Jesus healed a woman who was bound by Satan and was unable to straighten herself for eighteen years (v. 14), but he would not hesitate to untie his ox or donkey from the manger to lead it to the water on the Sabbath (v. 15). This is a very good case of self-deception. The synagogue ruler was upset because

22. Calvin, *Institutes* 1.1.2.
23. Bock, *Luke*, 1465.

the Sabbath was so flagrantly violated when keeping the Sabbath holy and not doing any work on it is one of the Ten Commandments, and violating it was a great sin worthy of death. All the while, he was conveniently forgetting that he had no qualms about breaking the Sabbath himself when it was expedient. Any work he had to do on the Sabbath had been readily rationalized and justified. So in the eyes of this synagogue ruler, Jesus was a lawbreaker and Sabbath desecrator, but he was a righteous and faithful law keeper, when in fact Jesus' healing was in perfect harmony with the intent of the Sabbath command, and the synagogue ruler's work on the Sabbath was not even though he had rationalized it. What Jesus was breaking and the synagogue ruler was keeping was not God's command but a man-made tradition. In this way, in the eyes of this hypocrite, a self-deceiver, his own unrighteous anger seemed righteous, but the righteous deed of Jesus seemed evil.

Matthew, who was especially concerned about the existence of self-deceived false believers in the church, uses the word *hypocrites* twelve times in his Gospel whereas Mark uses it only once and Luke twice. In the Sermon on the Mount, Jesus calls hypocrites those who give alms to be seen by others (Matt 6:2), pray in public to be seen (v. 5), and fast in a way others can see they are fasting (v. 16). These are examples of other-deception in presenting themselves as righteous when they are not, which aids their self-deception about their righteousness. Via comments, "The hypocrite may not intend to deceive, but he/she does lack integrity, correspondence between inner and outer, and is responsible for the lack because he/she has concealed the true nature of the inner person from herself/himself."[24]

In Matt 15:1–9, Pharisees and scribes confront Jesus for his disciples breaking the tradition of the elders by not washing their hands when they eat (vv. 1–2). Jesus responds to them by saying that they break God's commandment for the sake of their tradition (v. 3) and gives an example of their breaking the command to honor the parents by allowing people to not support their parents when they make an excuse of giving the money to God (vv. 4–6). Then Jesus calls them hypocrites, saying that Isaiah's prophecy in Isa 29:13 was fulfilled by them (vv. 8–9): "This people honors me with their lips, but their heart is far from me; in vain do they worship me, teaching as doctrines the commandments of men." In Matt 15, hypocrites are those who break God's commandment to keep man-made rules and consider themselves righteous.

---

24. Via, "Gospel of Matthew," 512.

In Matt 23 we find one of the most scathing rebukes by Jesus toward the scribes and Pharisees. Jesus repeatedly calls them hypocrites and pronounces woes on them for converting people to their beliefs that cannot save (vv. 13–15), for tithing meticulously but neglecting justice, mercy, and faithfulness (v. 23), for keeping the external appearances clean and beautiful but inwardly being filled with greed, self-indulgence, and all uncleanness (vv. 25–27), and for honoring the prophets and the righteous with their lips but in truth persecuting and killing them (vv. 29–34). Hypocrites, as the self-righteous in self-deception, will face God's judgment for their shedding of innocent blood (vv. 35–36).

John 8:33

The Gospel of John was written by the apostle John, who addresses himself as the beloved disciple in his Gospel (13:23; 19:26; 20:2; 21:7, 20). Some scholars today reject Johannine authorship of this Gospel. If the apostle John was not the one who wrote the Gospel and identified himself as the beloved disciple, it is hard to explain why the author mentions other disciples such as Peter, Andrew, Philip, Nathanael, Thomas, and both Judases but does not mention John and his brother James. Instead, the author mentions the "beloved disciple" in a prominent role alongside Peter, which is a role the apostle John plays in the other Gospels. Scholars generally agree that the author of the Gospel of John is the same author of 1–3 John because of many doctrinal, thematic, and linguistic similarities between them. The author of these epistles calls himself the elder (2 John 1; 3 John 1), and Eusebius in the fourth century AD believed this elder was a different person than the apostle John. Aside from the view of Eusebius, there was near unanimity among the church fathers in their belief that the apostle John was the author of the Gospel, the letters, and Revelation. The majority of evangelical scholars today agree. Apostle John is calling himself the elder in the epistles as the apostle Peter also identified himself as a fellow elder in his letter when he addressed the elders among his readers (1 Pet 5:1).

John's key verse is 20:31: "But these are written so that you may believe that Jesus is the Christ, the Son of God, and that by believing you may have life in his name." John shares his concern with Matthew about the presence of false believers in the believing community. John's letters (1–3 John) specifically address the false believers as those who had deficient belief in Jesus denying his humanity and yet were convinced that they were right, left John's church and started their own, and tried to win John's churches to their beliefs (1 John 2:18–19, 22; 4:1–3; 2 John 7).

In his Gospel, John addresses those who supposedly believed in Jesus but their faith turns out to be superficial. In 2:23–25, John mentions those who "believed in his name," but Jesus, knowing their hearts, did not entrust himself to them. Nicodemus is presented in chapter 3 as their representative who comes to Jesus professing a kind of faith (3:1–2), but Jesus tells him that he needs to be born again (3:3). John makes a clear connection between those with superficial faith in 2:23–25 and Nicodemus by using the expression "a man of the Pharisees named Nicodemus" in 3:1. John 2:25 ends with the word ἀνθρώπῳ (anthropo, "man"), and 3:1 begins with the words "there was a man of the Pharisees." That John is using the word *man* to connect Nicodemus with those who believed in Jesus but to whom Jesus did not entrust himself in 2:25 is clear because "man of the Pharisees" is an odd expression that only appears in John 3:1 and nowhere else in the Bible. John is introducing Nicodemus as one of those mentioned in 2:23–25 as having a superficial faith though they "believe in" Jesus in some way.

Nicodemus does acknowledge to Jesus that he believes that Jesus is a teacher who came from God and he could not perform his miracles unless God is with him (3:2). However, Jesus' response, that unless one is born again he cannot see the kingdom of God, indicates that Nicodemus is not born again at this point (3:3). As the Gospel narrative unfolds, John seems to indicate that Nicodemus went on to grow in his faith and became a genuine believer. Even though the word *faith* never appears in this Gospel, John uses the word *believe* eighty-four times, while Matthew, Mark, and Luke combined use the word thirty-two times. It shows that John wants to emphasize faith as a dynamic and continuous act of believing in Jesus, constantly acting and growing or falling away, not a static belief in a set of propositions. In John, those who fall away are false believers, since genuine believers are those whose salvation is secure as it is God's work, not of human effort or initiative (1:13; 6:37–40; 15:16).

In John 8:33 false believers are self-deceived about their supposed freedom when in fact they are enslaved to sin: "They answered him, 'We are offspring of Abraham and have never been enslaved to anyone. How is it that you say, "You will become free"?'" In John 8:30–59, Jesus speaks to many Jews who "believed in him" in a superficial way and yet turn out to still belong to the devil (v. 44, "you are of your father the devil") and not truly believe Jesus (v. 45, "But because I tell the truth, you do not believe me"). Referring to John 8:30 ("As he was saying these things, many believed in [ἐπίστευσαν εἰς (*episteusan eis*)] him"), Morris notes that the construction πιστεύω εἰς (*pisteuo eis*, "believe in") usually denotes trust in Jesus for salvation and is used for genuine disciples, but in this passage, the Jews addressed only made an outward profession, so Jesus' words to them are meant to drive home the meaning of true discipleship and real faith.[25] Though it is easy enough to be attracted to Jesus superficially, the test of genuine faith is "abiding," since only those who continue in Christ's words are genuine disciples.[26] As Carson points out, perseverance is the mark of true faith, of real disciples and what separates spurious faith from true faith, fickle disciples from genuine disciples.[27] Beasley-Murray believes that the purpose of John 8:31–59 is to expose the false belief.[28]

Though they claim to be free (v. 33), their accusation of Jesus as having a demon (vv. 48, 52) and their attempt to stone Jesus to death demonstrates that they are deep in their bondage to sin. Jesus tells them the truth about their condition, and they are enraged enough to try to kill him. Projects of self-deception feature an aversion to the truth, and they are sinful since an aversion to the truth is also an aversion to the God of the truth.[29] The characteristic aversion of self-deception, the turn away from truth, is parallel to the characteristic aversion of sin, the turn away from God.[30] It is not surprising then that these Jews tried to kill Jesus for telling them the truth about their sinfulness.

When John describes these people as "the Jews who had believed in him" (8:31), he is presenting them as false believers whose supposed faith in Jesus turns out to be only superficial. Jesus declares to them that their self-understanding as being offspring of Abraham and free is misguided or self-deceived since the truth is that their father is the devil who is the father of lies and a murderer (v. 44). Their response that Jesus is a Samaritan and has a demon (v. 48) reveals their true belief. They prove that their father is the devil and a murderer by attempting to murder Jesus when he declares to them that he is divine and that he existed before Abraham (v. 59).

---

25. Morris, *Gospel according to John*, 455.
26. Morris, *Gospel according to John*, 455–456.
27. Carson, *Gospels according to John*, 348.
28. Beasley-Murray, *John*, 132. Beasley-Murray lists Hoskyns, Bultmann, Henchen, and Becker as those who strongly advocate this view.
29. Wood, *Blaise Pascal on Duplicity*, 10.
30. Wood, *Blaise Pascal on Duplicity*, 11.

In John 2:23–25 and 8:31–59, John presents two different cases of false believers who both "believe in" Jesus superficially. In the former case, their faith still needs to grow and develop into saving faith, but as their representative Nicodemus shows, their prospect is hopeful. Many believe that Nicodemus eventually exhibited genuine faith when he stood up to defend Jesus against the chief priests and the Pharisees (John 7:50–52), and when he, along with Joseph of Arimathea, another disciple of Jesus, embalmed and buried Jesus (19:38–42). In the latter case, their initial "faith" turns hostile against Jesus when he confronts their sins and reveals his deity (8:58–59). So, John seems to present various kinds of faith in his Gospel, from the superficial faith that turns hostile to Jesus to the mature faith of those who worshiped Jesus (e.g., the man born blind in 9:38). The ultimate goal to which John wants to bring his readers seems to be Thomas' confession in 20:28: "My Lord and my God."

Acts 8:13

Though I grouped Acts of the Apostles with the Gospels in this book, Acts is in its own category. Its genre is often considered theological history since it narrates the history of the birth and expansion of the church in the first century from AD 30 to 60 from the perspective of not only a reliable historian but also a theologian, Luke, who conveys an important theological message through his historical narrative. Acts is the second volume of Luke's two-volume work of Luke-Acts, but it is separated from Luke in the Bible because the Gospel of John is placed after Luke since it is the last Gospel to be written among the four Gospels, and Luke is grouped with Matthew and Mark as the Synoptic Gospels that share so much in common.

In Acts 8:9–24, Luke tells the story of Simon the magician and his supposed conversion and subsequent rebuke and curse by Peter. Just as in Luke 8, John 2, and 8, though the word *believe* is used to describe Simon's faith, his interaction with Peter shows that Simon was a false believer who was in danger of eternal judgment.

When a great persecution broke out against the church in Jerusalem beginning with Saul's execution of Stephen (Saul being Paul's name before his conversion), the disciples were all scattered throughout Judea and Samaria. Philip, one of the seven deacons in the Jerusalem church (Acts 6:5), went to Samaria and evangelized the Samaritans, casting out demons and healing the sick. Many believed Philip and were baptized. One of them was

Simon, who used to amaze people with such powerful magic that people called him "the power of God called Great" (Acts 8:10b, translation mine). He was amazed by the signs and great miracles Philip performed, and Luke says that Simon believed, was baptized, and followed Philip (v. 13).

When the apostles in Jerusalem heard that Samaria had received the word of God, they sent their leaders, Peter and John, to them (8:14). There could be many reasons for this, and one of them probably was to maintain the unity in the body of Christ by making sure that the Samaritan believers would be part of the same church of Jesus Christ with the Jewish believers. The enmity between the Jews and the Samaritans was so strong that the unity between them even as believers was by no means guaranteed. This may be why God delayed giving the Holy Spirit to the Samaritan believers until the leaders in the Jerusalem church came down to Samaria, laid their hands on the Samaritans (which is a symbol of identification), and prayed for them (vv. 14–15). They had not previously received the Holy Spirit but were only baptized in Jesus' name (vv. 16–17). With this background, let's read verses 18–24 that describe what happens afterward:

> Now when Simon saw that the Spirit was given through the laying on of the apostles' hands, he offered them money, [19] saying, "Give me this power also, so that anyone on whom I lay my hands may receive the Holy Spirit." [20] But Peter said to him, "May your silver perish with you, because you thought you could obtain the gift of God with money! [21] You have neither part nor lot in this matter, for your heart is not right before God. [22] Repent, therefore, of this wickedness of yours, and pray to the Lord that, if possible, the intent of your heart may be forgiven you. [23] For I see that you are in the gall of bitterness and in the bond of iniquity." [24] And Simon answered, "Pray for me to the Lord, that nothing of what you have said may come upon me."

Luke does not tell us what happened to Simon after this exchange and leaves the story hanging. There are different views on Simon. Dillow believes that Simon was saved but was immature in his faith and fell into sin.[31] Another view held by Lenski is that Simon exercised genuine faith that was later perverted and lost.[32] Marshall similarly avers that though Simon was regenerate, Peter warned what would happen if he did not change his

---

31. Dillow, *Reign of the Servant Kings*, 327.
32. Lenski, *Interpretation of the Acts*, 322–27; cf. Marshall, *Acts*, 159.

attitude.³³ The third view is that Simon's faith was only superficial and never genuine.³⁴ There are good reasons to believe that the third view is the most probable one.

First, when the rest of the Samaritans received the Holy Spirit, Simon saw it (v. 18), meaning that he was an observer, not the recipient of the Holy Spirit as his subsequent behavior confirms.³⁵ His offer of money to purchase the power to confer the Spirit suggests that Simon saw what transpired before his eyes from a magician's perspective and as an opportunity for material gain. Second, a close parallel between Peter's condemnation of Simon and Paul's condemnation of Bar-Jesus Elymas in Acts 13 (8:21–23; 13:10) indicates that just as Bar-Jesus Elymas was an unbeliever, Luke is also portraying Simon as an unbeliever. Third, Peter tells Simon, "May your silver perish with you" (v. 20a); in Greek it says, τὸ ἀργύριόν σου σὺν σοὶ εἴη εἰς ἀπώλειαν (*to argyrion sou sun soi ei eis apoleian*, "to hell with you and your money," Phillips). The word ἀπώλειαν (*apoleian*, "destruction") is used in the New Testament eighteen times to denote eternal doom unless it is used of material things.³⁶ Fourth, Peter is uncertain about God's forgiveness of Simon (v. 22) because his heart is not right before God and Simon is in the gall of bitterness and the bond of iniquity (vv. 22–23), hardly a description of someone who just received the Holy Spirit. Fifth, in Luke's theology, how one handles money is an important indicator of one's spiritual condition. Simon's thought that the authority to give the Spirit is something to be bought and sold for profit is a strong indication that Luke is portraying him as not possessing the Spirit.³⁷ Sixth, given Luke's emphasis on the importance of the Holy Spirit in both Luke and Acts, to conclude that Simon, who received imprecation from Peter for offering money to buy the authority to give the Spirit, nevertheless possessed the Spirit, would be to ignore Luke's theology of the Holy Spirit. Seventh, the church fathers held that Simon was a heretic and the founder of a religious sect called Simonianism claiming his own divinity.³⁸ In the church tradition, Simon is represented

---

33. Marshall, *Acts*, 159.

34. Calvin, *Acts of the Apostles 1–13*, 233–41; Dunn, *Acts of the Apostles*, 109–10.

35. Dunn, *Acts of the Apostles*, 111: "Luke does not say that [Simon] received the Spirit but indicates that he saw it simply as a form of magic power."

36. See John 17:12; Rom 9:22; Phil 1:28; 3:19; 1 Tim 6:9; Heb 10:39; 2 Pet 2:1, 3; 3:16. The passages that most resemble the present one are Matt 7:13; 2 Thess 2:3; 2 Pet 3:7; and Rev 17:8. See Barrett, *Acts of the Apostles*, 413.

37. Blomberg, *Neither Poverty nor Riches*, 170.

38. E.g., Justin Martyr, *Apology* 1.26; Eusebius, *Historia Ecclesiastica* 2.13, 14;

Self-Deception in the New Testament

as a kind of hero among heretics—the personification of the anti-Christian principle. Irenaeus calls him "the master and progenitor of all heretics."[39] In short, Luke portrays Simon in Acts 8 as a false believer without the Holy Spirit who nevertheless "believed" and was baptized. If Simon was not just pretending to believe but believed in a superficial way, as Luke seems to portray him, then he would be another case of a self-deceived false believer. He would be an example of the third soil in the parable of the sower representing those who hear the word of God but whose worldly pursuits and desires choke out the word.

In the Gospels and Acts, we learn that the existence of self-deceived false believers in the believing communities is something the biblical writers accepted as a fact of life. They are not unbelievers since they profess faith in Jesus, but they are not genuinely regenerate believers either even though many of them consider themselves highly religious and deserving of a place in the kingdom of God. Some of them, like Nicodemus, can eventually become genuine believers provided they continue to grow in their faith from superficial faith to genuine faith, while others have the potential to become hostile to Jesus and his followers. We need to be mindful of the mixed nature of our congregations and provide teachings that clearly delineate the differences and similarities between genuine and false believers to help self-deceived false believers examine their faith and become genuine believers.

PAULINE EPISTLES

The apostle Paul wrote thirteen of twenty-seven books of the New Testament. Many believe him to be the most influential Christian of all time. Before he met the risen Jesus on the road to Damascus and became a follower of Christ, he was a Pharisee, convinced that Jesus could not have been the Messiah, and Christianity, or "the Way" (Acts 22:4; 24:14, 22), was a misguided and harmful cult that needed to be stopped and thwarted (Gal 1:13–14). He became a violent persecutor of Christians, but he considered himself blameless. Thus, Paul was a good case of a self-deceived person who failed in self-knowledge. He was opposing God and trying to destroy his work but thinking he was serving God: "as to zeal, a persecutor of the church; as to righteousness under the law, blameless" (Phil 3:6). As someone who had a first-hand experience of a self-deceived false believer, we can

---

Irenaeus, *Against Heresies* 1.27.

39. Irenaeus, *Against Heresies* 1.27.

expect Paul to show his concern for such people in the church such as the Judaizers who tried to force the Mosaic law as a requirement for salvation (e.g., Gal 5:2–5). That is exactly what we find in many of his letters. Paul has much to say about self-deception and false believers. Paul specifically mentions the "danger from false brothers" among the dangers he experienced in his ministry (2 Cor 11:26). We will examine many passages from Paul's letters.

Romans 1:18–23

Romans is considered by many as the most important letter in the New Testament because it presents the most detailed and formal account of the gospel and its implications, covering such important topics as revelation, sin, the righteousness of God, justification by faith, law and grace, election, Jew/gentile relationships, mission, and much more. Romans 1:18–23 states:

> For the wrath of God is revealed from heaven against all ungodliness and unrighteousness of men, who by their unrighteousness suppress the truth. [19] For what can be known about God is plain to them, because God has shown it to them. [20] For his invisible attributes, namely, his eternal power and divine nature, have been clearly perceived, ever since the creation of the world, in the things that have been made. So they are without excuse. [21] For although they knew God, they did not honor him as God or give thanks to him, but they became futile in their thinking, and their foolish hearts were darkened. [22] Claiming to be wise, they became fools, [23] and exchanged the glory of the immortal God for images resembling mortal man and birds and animals and creeping things.

In Rom 1 Paul states that people perceive the divine truth, but they suppress it because of their unrighteousness (vv. 18–20). Self-deception, according to Rom 1, is first volitional before it is cognitive. Because sinners choose to suppress the truth (v. 18), their thinking becomes futile and their foolish hearts darkened, and claiming to be wise, they become fools (vv. 21–22). "Where life is not experienced as a gift from God it has lost touch with reality and condemns itself to futility."[40]

The futility in thinking is the noetic effect of sin (or sin's effect on the mind)—the willful choice to reject God infects the mind to such a degree that human reasoning assumes a position that values creatures more than

---

40. Dunn, *Romans 1–8*, 60.

God.[41] Just as Adam and Eve believed the serpent rather than God, humanity exchanged the truth of God for a lie.[42] Self-deception, which involves a rational failure, is caused by a darkened heart, which is a moral failure by intentional choice (v. 21a, "For although they knew God, they did not honor him as God or give thanks to him ..."). Because self-deception is volitional, it is culpable. Three times Paul says that God has made known to man what can be known about God (1:19–20), and three times that humanity can know God and does experience him (vv. 19, 21, 32), but four times Paul asserts that they exchanged such knowledge for a counterfeit (vv. 23, 25, 26, 27).[43] Consequently, humanity has fallen into ingratitude, blindness, and rejection of God.[44] This failure to acknowledge God and know themselves as God's creatures is volitional and culpable—suppressing the truth of God, they recreate God in their image.

How do people suppress the truth? There are many different ways it can happen. They can avoid evidence by repressing memory or avoiding attention. They can also engage in the unconscious rationalization of their beliefs and behaviors. They can have unconscious desires and motives that steer them away from the truth. The suppression of the truth, for it to be successful, needs to happen at a subconscious level. There would be few, if any, who would admit that they are generally for a lie and against the truth. Thus, when Paul says that they knew God in 1:21, he must be referring to the knowledge that is kept in the dark by an intentional decision to replace the glory of God with that of creatures. Bird takes this knowledge of God to be an innate knowledge hardwired in human existence and a knowledge that comes from the creation.[45] Though people suppress the truth about God, it remains in their subconsciousness because God revealed himself to them through creation. As Fitzmyer points out, Paul "maintains that people can perceive or come to a certain awareness of God's 'eternal power and divinity' from reflection on what he has made evident in material creation."[46]

In the process of suppressing this knowledge of God, they claim to be wise when in fact they become fools (v. 22), which is another way of stating that they become self-deceived. As we have seen in our discussion

41. Bird, *Romans*, 56.
42. Bird, *Romans*, 56.
43. Edwards, *Romans*, 47.
44. Edwards, *Romans*, 47.
45. Bird, *Romans*, 55.
46. Fitzmyer, *Romans*, 273.

of self-deception in Proverbs, being wise in one's own eyes constitutes self-deception. Thus, in Rom 1 we see that self-deception happens intentionally and subconsciously. It involves faulty self-assessment ("claiming to be wise" in v. 22; cf. Prov 26:12) resulting in idolatry (v. 23). Dunn sees here an implicit allusion to the fall of Adam and Eve in Gen 3 as in both accounts we see a description of human aspiration for greater knowledge that actually results in a decline.[47]

When Paul describes those whose "foolish heart has been darkened" (1:23), this darkening of the heart has to do with spiritual and moral perception.[48] Romans 11:10 uses the same word σκοτίζω (*skotizo*, "darken") in a similar way but as a form of divine judgment ("let their eyes be darkened so that they cannot see, and bend their backs forever"; cf. 11:8, "God gave them a spirit of stupor, eyes that would not see and ears that would not hear, down to this very day"). In Rom 11:8 and 10, self-deception, the moral and spiritual failure to see the truth about ourselves because we decide to suppress the truth, happens as a result of divine judgment. God is sovereign in all things including our self-deception as we saw above when we discussed Isa 44:9–20.

Romans 1:18–32 makes a similar connection between self-deception and God's judgment on the sin of suppressing the truth—handing sinners over to their choice of sin and all its consequences. In verse 24, Paul says, "Therefore God gave them up in the lusts of their hearts to impurity," and in verse 26, "For this reason God gave them up to dishonorable passions." Then in verse 28, "And since they did not see fit to acknowledge God, God gave them up to a debased mind to do what ought not to be done." This has been true not only in the history of Israel as exemplified in the book of Judges but also in the history of the world. Thus, commenting on God's judgment in Romans, Moo cites the famous aphorism of Friedrich Schiller, a German historian and philosopher of the eighteenth century: "The history of the world is the judgment of the world."[49]

---

47. Dunn, *Romans 1–8*, 60. Fitzmyer disagrees and sees no echoes of Adam stories here (Fitzmyer, *Romans*, 274).

48. Bauer et al., *Greek-English Lexicon*, 932.

49. Moo, *Epistle to the Romans*, 101.

Romans 2:13

Romans 2:13 states, "For it is not the hearers of the law who are righteous before God, but the doers of the law who will be justified," sounding very much like Jas 2:24 ("You see that a person is justified by works and not by faith alone"). In Jas 2:14–26, James addresses a nominal Christian who claims to have faith but his lack of works (i.e., manifestations of his faith) proves that his faith is dead, similar to the faith of the demons who believe that God is one. This is a belief in the sound doctrine of monotheism (Jas 2:18–19), but their "faith" cannot save them. Elsewhere in his letter, James addresses self-deception more specifically (1:16, 22, 26). We will discuss these later.

In Rom 2, Paul mentions that a Jew may consider himself to be a teacher of the law and the truth (vv. 17–20), but if he is not a doer of the law, his identity as a Jew and his circumcision only aid his self-deception about his status as righteous before God since a true Jew in God's sight is the one who has circumcision of the heart by the Spirit (v. 29, "But a Jew is one inwardly, and circumcision is a matter of the heart, by the Spirit, not by the letter"). In the case of a Jew who fails to be a doer of the law and remains a hearer only, he is self-deceived. Unlike his self-assessment, he is not a true Jew since he is without the Spirit and without the true circumcision of the heart (v. 28, "For no one is a Jew who is merely one outwardly, nor is circumcision outward and physical").

Dan O. Via talks about Paul's own self-deception before conversion when he considered himself a blameless Jew but with some nagging awareness of his sinfulness and hypocrisy:

> The moral fault and the failure to achieve life through obedience (Romans 7) must have been to some degree inaccessible to him in order to account for his good conscience (blamelessness) in Phil. 3:4–9. But it must also have been to some degree conscious in order to account for the anxious zeal with which he continued to pursue the righteousness of the law (Phil. 3:4–6; Gal. 1:13–14; Rom. 10:2). The failure also needs to be regarded as partially conscious in order to explain why one would have reason to turn to the offer of salvation in the gospel. How could or why would one respond to a new possibility if the old life seemed to be unproblematic? Paul both believes and disbelieves the cover story that he is blameless. He both disbelieves and believes the real story that his own righteousness is refuse (Phil. 3:8) and that he does evil (Rom. 7:18–19). . . . These considerations point us to the motive or dynamic for self-deception suggested by Paul. We conceal the

truth from ourselves, do not spell it out, because we want to be blameless in our own eyes, want to be justified, on the basis of an effort that is our own (Rom. 10:2–3; Phil. 3:3–9). It has been suggested that the anxious desire to be what we want to be disposes us to believe that we actually are: this is simply the way the human mind works. Paul would qualify this by adding, No, this is the way the fallen mind, the mind of the flesh, works.[50]

Like Paul before salvation, the Jews Paul describes in Rom 2 depended on the false security that they had a relationship with God and knew his will while disavowing the awareness that the law calls for action, which they failed to do.[51] In 2:17–24, Paul describes them this way:

> [17] But if you call yourself a Jew and rely on the law and boast in God [18] and know his will and approve what is excellent, because you are instructed from the law; [19] and if you are sure that you yourself are a guide to the blind, a light to those who are in darkness, [20] an instructor of the foolish, a teacher of children, having in the law the embodiment of knowledge and truth— [21] you then who teach others, do you not teach yourself? While you preach against stealing, do you steal? [22] You who say that one must not commit adultery, do you commit adultery? You who abhor idols, do you rob temples? [23] You who boast in the law dishonor God by breaking the law. [24] For, as it is written, "The name of God is blasphemed among the Gentiles because of you."

The obedience of the heart is what God requires, but they deceive themselves into believing that external obedience is enough.[52] But external obedience without the obedience of the heart only leads to self-deception. Perhaps the reason why Jesus was so harsh in his pronouncement of judgment on the Pharisees and the scribes (Matt 23:1–36; Luke 11:37–52) was that those harsh words were necessary to awaken them out of their self-deception. They believed that they were pious and righteous, having God's approval upon them—all the while inwardly filled with hypocrisy and lawlessness (Matt 23:28), preventing themselves and their converts from entering the kingdom of God (v. 13), and facing dire consequences of eternal punishment.

---

50. Via, *Self-Deception and Wholeness*, 27.
51. Via, *Self-Deception and Wholeness*, 45.
52. Via, *Self-Deception and Wholeness*, 45.

When Paul says in Phil 3:6 that he was blameless before the law, Coe analyzes the psychology of such a claim:

> In Philippians 3, apostle Paul reflects upon his own distorted, pre-converted self-concept that was plagued by autonomy and self righteousness. . . . We should not kid ourselves about Paul's psychological profile prior to conversion. Here is an individual quite full of himself, killing others in the name of a projected deity, in the image of his own need, all as a prop to support his false self and identity. Freud's view of God as a projection of a human need is quite true of Paul, and of false religion in general.[53]

This assessment of Paul may sound harsh, but Coe's argument that Paul's self-deceived self-image led to his creation of a false god rings true and is helpful to understand the Jewish leaders of Jesus' days, all religious leaders in Israel who persecuted God's prophets, and more broadly, all false religions. There is an appearance of godliness but with no reality to it (cf. 2 Tim 3:5), and that was probably a contributing factor to Paul's conversion to Christianity.

Romans 7:13—8:17

In Rom 7:13–25, Paul recounts his utter failure in his struggle against sin as he attempted to obey the law as a Jew without the Spirit's empowerment. But in Phil 3:6, he claims that he was blameless as to the righteousness under the law. As a Jew, Paul had both a cover story of his blameless obedience to the law regarding external observance and a real story of inner struggle against sin and utter helplessness against its enslavement. Sin deceives man concerning the law, distorting it, imposing a false understanding of it, and suggesting that man is in a position to fulfill it, which all leads to self-righteousness. Thus, sin by deception succeeds in accomplishing man's death by means of that which God gave for life.[54] After his conversion and regeneration by the Spirit, Paul could look back at his former life as a Jew and see that his sinful nature (Paul calls it "body of death" in Rom 7:24) was enslaving him to sin though he delighted in the law of God, and only the Spirit of God could set him free from the law of sin and death (Rom 8:1).

---

53. Coe, "Intentional Spiritual Formation," 92.
54. Cranfield, *Romans 1–8*, 353.

Scholars are divided in their interpretations of Rom 7:13–25, some holding that Paul is describing his Christian experience and others believing that Paul is relaying his life as a Jew before his regeneration and empowerment by the Holy Spirit. No matter which view they take, most believers can identify with struggling with sin and feeling helpless about it when they do not seek the Holy Spirit's help.[55] I believe that Paul is describing the helpless struggle against sin by the unregenerate including the false believers. Keener sees the contrasts between Paul's descriptions in Rom 7:7–25 with the larger context too great to fit the Christian life even if Paul considered himself an unusually weak Christian: law, sin, and death (7:7–13) versus freed from law (7:4, 6; 8:2), sin (6:18, 20, 22), and death (5:21; 6:23; 8:2); I am fleshy (7:14) versus you are not in the (sphere of) flesh, if Christ lives in you (8:9), and no longer in the flesh (7:5); I have been sold under (as a slave to) sin (7:14; cf. 7:23) versus believers have been freed from enslavement to sin (6:18, 20, 22), and they are "redeemed" (3:24); knowing right (in the law) without the ability to do right (7:15–23) versus power to live righteously (8:4); sin dwells in (and rules) me (7:17, 20) versus the Spirit dwells in believers (8:9, 11); nothing good dwells in me (i.e., in me as flesh; 7:18) versus the Spirit dwells in believers (8:9, 11); the law of sin dominates his bodily members (7:23) versus believers are freed from the law of sin (8:2); sin wins the war and captures "me" as a prisoner (7:23) versus believers can win the spiritual war (2 Cor 10:3–5); a slave to the law of sin in his flesh (7:25) versus believers are freed from the law of sin (8:2; 6:18, 20, 22).[56]

If Paul is describing his pre-conversion experience in Rom 7:13–25, as I believe he is, why does he use the present tense in describing his struggles against sin? After surveying several different interpretations of the identity of "I" in Rom 7:7–25, Kruse concludes that the view that is receiving increasingly wider support is the one that holds that "I" denotes the experience of Israel as a nation.[57] According to this interpretation, Paul is adopting the rhetorical device of speech-in-character recognized by early church fathers in their exposition of Rom 7.[58] The reason the tense switches from the aorist (a Greek past tense) in verses 7–13 to the present in verses 14–25 is that the former describes Israel's historical encounter with the law

---

55. Cf. Moo, *Epistle to the Romans*, 445–51.
56. Keener, *Romans*.
57. Kruse, *Paul's Letter to the Romans*, 316–21.
58. Kruse, *Paul's Letter to the Romans*, 316–21.

at Sinai and the latter Israel's ongoing experience of life under the law.[59] The autobiographical overtones of the passages are understood as Paul identifying his own pre-Christian experience with that of Israel.[60] Liubinskas sees both the experience of Israel and Adam and Eve in this passage and Paul drawing all of humanity "under the rubric of sin's hijacking of God's holy, just, and good law for its own evil purposes (vv. 12–13). It is this experience that is common to both Jewish and gentile human families."[61]

Does it mean that the experience Paul depicts in Rom 7:14–25 does not apply to regenerate believers at all? Even the most mature believers have experienced being defeated by the dominating power of sin because of the sinful nature they have inherited, or as Paul puts it, "I am of the flesh, sold under sin" (7:14) while they live in this interim period of already/not yet. The kingdom of God and its redemptive and liberating power have already been inaugurated with Christ's death and resurrection, but its full redemption and liberation from sin and death await his second coming. So Rom 7:14–25 applies to all human struggle against sin and failure when pursued apart from the liberating power of the Holy Spirit. The difference between the unregenerate and regenerate people is nevertheless huge. For the unregenerate, enslavement to sin is the way of life with no escape, but for the regenerate, it can always be broken because the empowering power of the Spirit is readily available. Paul's description of enslavement to sin therefore concerns the unregenerate though is applicable to the regenerate when they do not rely on the Holy Spirit.

Would it also be possible that Paul has self-deceived false believers in mind in Rom 7:14–25 and is identifying with their experiences? Could he be using the present tense to depict their present struggles with sin though they consider themselves believers? Paul may be using first-person pronouns to represent the experiences of those in the church who "serve the law of God with my mind, but with my flesh I serve the law of sin" (7:25). After all, Paul is mindful of their existence in his churches, and he is concerned about them as he himself had a first-hand experience of being a self-deceived believer in God as a former Pharisee.

Paul uses a hypothetical or rhetorical "I" in 1 Cor 10:29–30; 13:1–3, 11–12, and the present tense verbs would serve to accentuate rhetorical vividness similar to the use of the historical present (using the present tense

---

59. Kruse, *Paul's Letter to the Romans*, 316–21.

60. Kruse, *Paul's Letter to the Romans*, 316–21; cf. Schreiner, *Romans*, 362.

61. Liubinskas, *Ethnographic Character of Romans*, 175.

to describe past events) in Mark's Gospel.[62] The reason why there is no condemnation for those who are in Christ Jesus (not just anyone in the church, but those in Christ) is that the law of the Spirit of life has set them free from the law of sin and death (8:1–2). The righteous requirement of the law can only be fulfilled in those who walk not according to the flesh but according to the Spirit (8:4) because the mind that is set on the flesh is hostile to God and cannot submit to God's law (8:7; 7:13–25).[63]

In 7:22, Paul mentions that he delights in the law of God in his inner being, but in 8:7 he says that the mind that is set on the flesh is hostile to God. Can these two states exist simultaneously in the same person? Yes, this is the way a self-deceived person operates—there is a cover story that operates in the conscious mind and a true story underneath it. As a zealous Jew, Paul delighted in the law of God, and his whole life was dedicated to obeying the law and attaining righteousness through it. But the truth was that his mind was hostile to God because he was seeking to establish his own righteousness through the law, and he did not submit to God's righteousness (Rom 10:3). That is how he ended up persecuting those who followed Christ, the incarnate God the Son.

In his righteousness that he believed he achieved by obeying the law, Paul the Pharisee could not believe that Jesus was the Jewish Messiah who came to fulfill the law because he defied much of the law and was cursed by God according to the law since he was hanged on a tree (Gal 3:13 quoting Deut 21:23). Paul must have concluded that Jesus was one of those self-claimed false messiahs (and there were many in the first century) and his followers must be stopped. Paul was zealous for God and the law, but he was in the flesh without the Spirit, and ironically he was fulfilling the prophecy made by Jesus: "They will put you out of the synagogues. Indeed, the hour is coming when whoever kills you will think he is offering service to God" (John 16:2). In Paul's own words, "For the mind that is set on the flesh is hostile to God, for it does not submit to God's law; indeed, it cannot" (Rom 8:7). Without the Spirit, Paul's mind was set on the flesh even when he was trying to obey and protect the law.

Only those who have the Spirit of Christ are not in the flesh but in the Spirit (8:9). Paul states in 8:10, "But if Christ is in you, although the body is dead because of sin, the Spirit is life because of righteousness." Here, the words "the body is dead because of sin" do not mean that Christians are

---

62. Keener, *Romans*, 91–93.
63. Keener, *Romans*, 91–93.

enslaved to sin, because verses 10 and 11 are not talking about believers' enslavement to sin but about the effect of sin on all humanity and the Spirit's resurrection power for the believers. Paul never describes being enslaved to sin as the body being dead because of sin. In verse 10, Paul is simply contrasting the reality of death-resulting flesh through sin and life-resulting Spirit and the righteousness that the Spirit produces—the contrast is between the flesh and the Spirit. Christians are not immune from the sinful nature they inherit from their parents, but the Spirit in them will overcome the deathly effect of sinful nature they still possess: "If the Spirit of him who raised Jesus from the dead dwells in you, he who raised Christ Jesus from the dead will also give life to your mortal bodies through his Spirit who dwells in you" (8:11). Paul goes on to warn that those who live according to the flesh will die, and those who put to death the deeds of the body will live (8:13), declaring that children of God are those who are led by the Spirit of God (8:14).

So Paul is clearly distinguishing between those who are in the flesh living according to the sinful nature without the Spirit and those who are putting to death the deeds of the body with the help of the Holy Spirit. The contrast is between the unregenerate and the regenerate. Within the church, the contrast is between the false believers and the genuine believers, and Paul seems to be contrasting these two groups. The fact that Paul repeatedly emphasizes the indwelling and leading of the Holy Spirit in a letter to a Christian community suggests that he was keenly aware of the possibility of belonging to a believing community without being indwelt by the Spirit: "Anyone who does not have the Spirit of Christ does not belong to him" (8:9b). This is consistent with the earlier observation that Jesus anticipated, and the New Testament writers understood, the church to be a mixed community of genuine and false believers.

If the possibility of belonging to a believing community but not having the Spirit was not a concern in Paul's mind, it is difficult to understand why Paul uses four conditional clauses in a context in which he is teaching the prominent role of the Spirit in a believer's life: "if in fact the Spirit of God dwells in you" (8:9a), "if Christ is in you" (8:10a), "if the Spirit of him who raised Jesus from the dead dwells in you" (8:11a), and "if by the Spirit you put to death the deeds of the body, you will live" (8:13b). Why didn't Paul employ much more affirmative and stronger assertions that would assure them that they indeed have the Spirit? Why did he allow them to raise questions about the Spirit's presence in them? There is no satisfactory explanation for it except that the possibility of belonging to a believing community without having the Spirit was a real one in Paul's mind. Thus, instead of defining a believer as someone who belongs to a believing community or who believes in a set of doctrines, Paul defines her or him as someone who has the Spirit of Christ (8:14).

Any argument that because Paul is using first class conditional clauses, these conditional clauses should be translated not as conditions but as statements ("since in fact the Spirit of God dwells in you" [8:9a], "since Christ is in you" [8:10a], etc.) does not stand scrutiny.[64] In 8:13a, Paul states, "For if you live according to the flesh you will die." According to this view, this statement should be translated, "For since you live according to the flesh you will die." No one would agree with such a translation since it is clear from the context that Paul is not saying that. He is contrasting two conditions and their consequences in verse 13: "For if you live according to the flesh you will die, but if by the Spirit you put to death the deeds of the body, you will live." Replacing "if" with "since" in this verse will make no sense. Contrary to the popular notion that first class conditional clauses in Greek grammar assume facts and therefore "if" can be translated as "since," the fact is that they only assume truth for the sake of argument.[65] Whether they are stating facts can only be determined by the context. In only 37 percent of the instances of the first class condition in the New Testament, "if" can be translated as "since."[66] Especially when there are two opposed conditional statements (as is the case of Rom 8:13), "if" cannot possibly be translated "since."[67]

Dunn remarks, "In what amounts to the nearest thing to a definition of 'Christian' in his writings, Paul defines a Christian, albeit in negative formulation, as one who has the Spirit of Christ."[68] Fee translates Rom 8:9 this way: "If anyone does not have the Spirit, that person does not belong to Christ at all."[69] In contrast, the Spirit in a genuine believer makes her cry out, "Abba, Father," and assures her that she is God's child, and enables her to suffer with Christ as his joint heir (8:15–17). Often, it is persecution

---

64. In Greek grammar, we have a first class conditional clause when a conditional statement uses εἰ (*ei*, "if") with the indicative mood verb in the protasis.
65. Wallace, *Greek Grammar*, 690.
66. Wallace, *Greek Grammar*, 690.
67. Wallace, *Greek Grammar*, 690.
68. Dunn, *Romans 1–8*, 444.
69. Fee, *Paul, the Spirit*, 89.

and suffering that separate genuine and false believers as trials test the genuineness of their faith (8:18–25; cf. Jas 1:2–4; 1 Pet 1:7).

1 Corinthians 3:18

First Corinthians is one of at least four letters Paul wrote to the church in Corinth that he planted in the 50s. Two letters, 1 and 2 Corinthians, survived and the other two did not. In 1 Cor 5:9, Paul refers to a previous letter he wrote to them ("I wrote to you in my letter not to associate with sexually immoral people"). Then in 2 Cor 2:3, Paul refers to another letter he wrote between 1 and 2 Corinthians: "And I wrote as I did, so that when I came I might not suffer pain from those who should have made me rejoice, for I felt sure of all of you, that my joy would be the joy of you all."

The fact that Paul wrote at least four letters to the church in Corinth indicates that there were many issues in this church that necessitated Paul's attention. This church probably ranked among the top churches that caused Paul's greatest concerns. Some of the problems that the church was experiencing included divisions (1 Cor 1:10–13; 3:1–5), worldly wisdom (3:18–23), immorality (5:1–12; 6:9–10, 12–20), lawsuits against believers (6:1–8), eating food sacrificed to idols (8:1–13), idolatry (10:1–22), disorderly worship (11:2–16; 14:1–40), divisive Lord's Supper practices (11:17–34), denial of bodily resurrection (15:12–19), rejection of Paul's apostleship (2 Cor 6:12; 7:2; 10:7–10), and false apostles (2 Cor 11:1–29). Among a host of problems the church was facing in Corinth, one was that of false apostles who preached a different gospel (2 Cor 11:4). Paul calls them "deceitful workmen, disguising themselves as apostles of Christ" and as "servants of righteousness" just as Satan disguises himself as an angel of light (11:13–14). Deception has always been a key tactic of Satan from the very beginning of human history (cf. Gen 3). Jesus describes him this way: "When he lies, he speaks out of his own character, for he is a liar and the father of lies" (John 8:44).

In such a context, it is not surprising that Paul addressed the issue of self-deception in 1 and 2 Corinthians. In 1 Cor 3:18, Paul admonishes, "Do not deceive yourselves. If any of you think you are wise by the standards of this age, you should become fools so that you may become wise." This admonition follows his rebuke of their immaturity exhibited through their jealousy and strife as they were forming factions of Paul's party and Apollos's party (3:1–4). Paul presents self-deception as a key concept here, and that is why many English translations translate the third-person imperative in Greek (literally, "let no one deceive himself") as a second-person imperative, "do not deceive yourselves" (e.g., NRSV, NIV, Collins).[70] Paul expresses one of Socrates' best-known maxims that recognition of one's own ignorance is the starting point for knowledge or wisdom.[71] Considering oneself wise using worldly standards is self-deception because worldly wisdom is folly with God (v. 19). Proverbs has repeated warnings against being wise in one's own eyes, and Paul issues warnings against self-deception elsewhere in 1 Cor 6:9; 15:33; and Gal 6:3 and 7. He says something similar in 1 Cor 8:2: "If anyone imagines that he knows something, he does not yet know as he ought to know."

Confidence of the Corinthians in their wisdom needed to be discouraged and recognized as self-deception because wrong standards were used to gain such confidence and it was producing divisions in the church, clearly demonstrating that they were not wise. True wisdom would accompany humility and promote unity, not division. But for such recognition to take place, the gospel is needed to bring light (2 Cor 4:6) and knowledge (Phil 3:8) and disclose the secrets and purposes of the heart (1 Cor 4:5; 14:25), so a unifying wholeness of the self may be achieved.[72] Paul wants the Corinthian believers to realize that when they divide the church, it is not wisdom but carnality and spiritual immaturity (3:3). To the degree they considered themselves wise while forming parties that divided the church, they were self-deceived (3:18–23). On judgment day, their work with all their hidden agendas and motives will be tested by fire and will be revealed: "each one's work will become manifest, for the Day will disclose it, because it will be revealed by fire, and the fire will test what sort of work each one has done" (3:13). In the Corinthian church, self-deception was causing the believers to divide the church by forming factions while believing that they were wise and doing what was right.

1 Corinthians 4:5

In 1 Cor 4:5, Paul states, "Therefore do not pronounce judgment before the time, before the Lord comes, who will bring to light the things now hidden in darkness and will disclose the purposes of the heart. Then each one

---

70. Thiselton, *First Epistle to the Corinthians*, 321.
71. Thiselton, *First Epistle to the Corinthians*, 321.
72. Via, *Self-Deception and Wholeness*, 47.

will receive his commendation from God." In dealing with the Corinthians, sometimes Paul was forced to defend his apostleship and ministry because some in the church of Corinth were questioning his apostleship (e.g., 1 Cor 4:18–20). There seems to be Jewish parallelism at work in the phrase "bring to light things that are now hidden and will disclose the purpose of the heart," meaning that bringing to light things that are now hidden is equated to disclosing the purpose of the heart. If so, then Paul is echoing what Jeremiah said in 17:9 that the heart is deceitful and no one can know what is hidden in it except God. Paul is not aware of anything against himself, but he is not thereby acquitted since it is the Lord who judges him (1 Cor 4:4). Paul knows that just because he is not aware of any wrongdoing on his part, that does not necessarily mean that he is guiltless, because he could be unaware of his guilt or self-deceived about his innocence. Paul knows that the human heart, before its full restoration on the last day, is perfectly capable of deceiving the most conscientious and devoted followers of Jesus Christ like himself. Paul uses "heart" to "signify the hidden motives, desires, and interests which may even deceive himself, and of which the self is certainly not fully aware."[73] Because of the possibility of self-deception about what is hidden in our hearts, Paul says that we need to let God be our judge (v. 4) and not others (v. 5), not even ourselves (v. 3).

How can we apply this to our lives? For one, too much introspection and self-doubt may not be helpful. After some thoughtful self-reflection, we should hand over the matter to God and let him be the judge of our deepest motives that are not accessible to us. For example, when I decided to leave my ministry at Global Mission Church of Greater Washington in Silver Spring, Maryland, in 2008 to take up a full-time teaching position at Taylor University in Upland, Indiana, where I still teach currently, I was a full-time associate pastor in charge of family ministry, discipleship training ministry, Stephen Ministry, and Evangelism Explosion ministry, among other things at this three thousand–member Korean-American church. I was also an adjunct professor at Southern Baptist Theological Seminary, Silver Spring extension, teaching Greek and Hebrew classes. In short, I had a very fulfilling ministry, and, I might add, a fruitful one.

So, when I decided to leave it all, I had to make sure that it was from the Lord. But it was impossible to be completely free from self-doubts about my motives and inner desires: Was I making this move because of selfish desires? How about all the people I was leaving behind who I knew were

---

73. Thiselton, *First Epistle to the Corinthians*, 343.

benefiting from my ministry? In the end, I had to leave the ultimate judgment to God and be willing to let him reveal the hidden purpose of my heart on the day of judgment. I knew I made the decision after seeking God's will for quite some time in prayers, and I also knew that the passion of my heart was investing my life into the leaders of the next generation in a full-time teaching capacity at an undergraduate institution. Beyond that, I let God be the judge of the hidden agendas and ulterior motives of my heart since I don't have access to them for now.

The same thing can be said about criticism from others. It is impossible to be free from criticism not only from the public but also from even the closest members of your family when they do not agree with your decision. When I left Silver Spring, Maryland, where my church was, to go to Upland, Indiana, to teach at Taylor, my older daughter was strongly against the decision because she did not want to leave behind all her friends whom she worked very hard to make (she was a ninth grader) and because I did not discuss it with her when I decided to move. When my family went to Taylor for my campus interview, she could not come with us because she was on a mission trip. So when my family discussed whether I should accept the teaching position after the campus interview, she was not there. She became so upset with me and God that she even left her faith. Sixteen years later, as I am writing this book in 2024, she still has not returned to God. So, did I make the right decision when I left my church? I believe I was following the Lord's leading, and I am convinced that I am in the middle of God's will here at Taylor University, a wonderful Christian higher education institution. But that is the best I can do. I need to leave the rest to the Lord to judge. Though the return of my daughter to her faith is the greatest burden of my soul and daily prayer, it does not help me to do more soul-searching and have self-doubts.

1 Corinthians 6:9

In 1 Cor 6:9, Paul warns that anyone who lives in habitual sin and thinks that he will inherit the kingdom of God is self-deceived: "Or do you not know that the unrighteous will not inherit the kingdom of God? Do not be deceived: neither the sexually immoral, nor idolaters, nor adulterers, nor men who practice homosexuality, nor thieves, nor the covetous, nor drunkards, nor revilers, nor swindlers, will inherit the kingdom of God." Paul's concern is that the Corinthians must stop deceiving themselves, or allowing themselves to be deceived.[74] Similarly, in Gal 6:7 Paul warns against the self-deception of thinking that one will not have to face the consequences of his choices: "Do not be deceived: God cannot be mocked. A man reaps what he sows." Both 1 Cor 6:9 and Gal 6:7 reveal the gravity of the consequence of self-deception. The self-deceived in 1 Cor 6:9 are deceived in their false hope that they will inherit the kingdom of God; unfortunately, no less than their eternal destiny is at stake.

The warning is addressed to those who are professing believers in a church Paul planted. Even a church planted by Paul himself could not be free from the existence of false believers in its midst. They accepted Paul's teaching of the word of God and became members of an apostolic church. The Corinthian church experienced God's power and boasted about its spiritual gifts (1 Cor 12, 14). No wonder they were looking forward to inheriting the kingdom of God. So, Paul's dire warning that those who were practicing habitual sin may not inherit the kingdom of God probably came as a shock to many.

The fact that they were boastful about a member having an incestuous relationship with his father's wife (1 Cor 5:1–2) shows that they were not bothered by the practice of immorality. They also seemed to have denied the bodily resurrection and instead only believed in spiritual resurrection (1 Cor 15:12, "Now if Christ is proclaimed as raised from the dead, how can some of you say that there is no resurrection of the dead?"). This indicates that they were influenced by Greek dualism that considered the matter including the body as evil or at least inconsequential, leading to a view that what one does in the body is irrelevant since God will eventually destroy it. Paul recites one of their slogans in 1 Cor 6:13a: "Food is for the stomach and the stomach for food, and God will destroy them both" (translation mine). So do whatever you want with your body and fulfill its desires. Do you want to have your father's wife? Go ahead. We know that it does not matter what we do with our bodies since they will eventually be gone. There is no bodily resurrection, only a spiritual one that already happened when we were saved. Such an idea was later developed in the second century into full-blown Gnosticism, and some in the Corinthian church seemed to have embraced its incipient form. Paul had to deconstruct this false belief and teach them that what they do in their bodies is not only consequential but indicative of their inheritance of the kingdom of God. To think otherwise would be to engage in self-deception.

---

74. Fee, *First Epistle to the Corinthians*, 242.

What the Bible Says about the Dangers of Self-Deception

At Taylor University, when I talk about biblical assurance of salvation, I ask students every semester this question using a digital survey device that can take anonymous polls and show immediate results: "What percentage of people in our churches do you think are self-deceived false believers?" I have been asking this question for more than sixteen years, and students' responses are strikingly consistent. The average percentage that students consistently come up with is about 50 percent. Every semester, students tell me that they think about half the people who go to church and profess their faith are self-deceived false believers. I am not surprised by such a response since, after all, Jesus himself, when asked by his disciples, "Lord, will those who are saved be few?" (Luke 13:23), replied by saying, "Strive to enter through the narrow door. For many, I tell you, will seek to enter and will not be able" (v. 24). We already saw in Matthew that Jesus' response to many who call him "Lord" on the day of his judgment will be, "I never knew you" (Matt 7:23). The existence of self-deceived false believers in churches today even up to half of the makeup of a church is in the radar of young Christians.

I am not saying this in a judgmental spirit but out of concern. We send our missionaries to the remotest parts of the world to save souls and make disciples in obedience to the Great Commission of our Lord (Matt 28:19–20). How tragic would it be then when we find out that we failed to help those who were right here with us in our churches? We must realize that church is also a mission field, and we must be strategic about reaching the unregenerated in our midst. Sermons, Bible studies, ministries, and small groups of our churches should be designed with the existence of self-deceived false believers in mind and with strategies to help them come to the saving knowledge of Jesus Christ.

The most important thing in this endeavor is to teach the whole counsel of God (Acts 20:27) since the word of God is able to build people up and give them "the inheritance among all those who are sanctified" (v. 32). It is important to teach the congregation what the Bible says about genuine believers and false believers, about the need for perseverance through temptations and trials so the word of God can take root in their hearts and bear fruit resulting in salvation and spiritual growth (cf. 1 Cor 15:2; Col 1:21–23).

2 Corinthians 13:5–7

Second Corinthians 13:5–7 states:

> Examine yourselves, to see whether you are in the faith. Test yourselves. Or do you not realize this about yourselves, that Jesus Christ is in you?—unless indeed you fail to meet the test! ⁶ I hope you will find out that we have not failed the test. ⁷ But we pray to God that you may not do wrong—not that we may appear to have met the test, but that you may do what is right, though we may seem to have failed.

In verse 5, Paul challenges the believers in Corinth to examine themselves to see if they are in the faith. Paul often uses the expression "the faith" with the sense of the belief, convictions, and the whole practice of following Christ.[75] The assumption that underlies Paul's challenge is that if they are genuine believers then they will perceive that Jesus Christ is in them (thus authenticating Paul's apostleship). Whether by this self-examination Paul intended a search for the evidence of change in one's life, the internal witness of the Spirit, or some other evidence is not stated, but one thing is clear—this test is a subjective one. The test was whether the Corinthians perceived that Jesus Christ was in them by examining themselves. Christ's indwelling presence in believers is a reality that Paul expected believers to recognize by self-examination. The verb πειράζετε (*peirazete*), translated as "examine" in verse 5, speaks of making a critical examination of something to determine its genuineness.[76] Paul does not automatically assume that if someone is in the church, he or she must be a genuine believer. In Rom 8:9, 17; 11:22; and Col 1:22–23, Paul attaches a condition for someone to be in Christ. For example, Col 1:22–23a states, "he has now reconciled in his body of flesh by his death, in order to present you holy and blameless and above reproach before him, if indeed you continue in the faith, stable and steadfast, not shifting from the hope of the gospel that you heard." He does the same thing in 2 Cor 13:5 when he adds a condition, "unless indeed you fail to meet the test!" or more literally, "unless you are ἀδόκιμοί (*adokimoi*)." We will return to this important word shortly.

Both Calvin and Luther address the importance of the subjective witness of the Holy Spirit. For example, Calvin states: "For as God alone can properly bear witness to His own words, so those words cannot obtain full credit in the heart of man until they are sealed by the inward testimony of the Spirit."[77] In Calvin's view, it is the work of the Holy Spirit, not human

---

75. Guthrie, *2 Corinthians*, 638.
76. Guthrie, *2 Corinthians*, 638.
77. Calvin, *Institutes* 1.7.4.

reason, that enables a person to truly understand and believe the gospel message. Luther taught that one can believe the gospel truth without the enablement of the Holy Spirit and yet that is not sufficient. For Luther, if one believes that only Christ can take away his sins, it is not enough unless it is the Spirit who caused him to believe this.[78] Time and again Luther emphasizes that it is not sufficient to accept the teaching of the Scriptures and the church about Christ as correct since even the demons and ungodly men believe in this manner.[79]

Zwingli, another key figure in the Reformation movement, also states that "it is the Holy Spirit who inwardly gives the certainty that is an integral component of saving faith. The election of others is a matter hidden from us, but to us the Spirit personally gives a certainty of our own election and salvation. This is a result of the drawing of the Father . . . and so is the gift of God."[80] The indwelling Spirit gives assurance to genuine believers that they are children of God in a way that no outside source can. It also enables them to live out their lives in a way that is consistent with their profession of faith, which is another mark of genuine believers.

Returning to the word ἀδόκιμοί (adokimoi), it is a plural form of ἀδόκιμος (adokimos) which basically means a "counterfeit," or "tested and proven false." It appears eight times in the New Testament, three times in 2 Cor 13:5–7, and five times elsewhere. It is worthwhile to examine those five appearances. In Rom 1:28, it means "debased." The verbal form δοκιμάζω (dokimazo) appears in the same verse, meaning "approve." The verse states, "And since they did not see fit to acknowledge (or approve) God, God gave them up to a debased (ἀδόκιμον, adokimon) mind to do what ought not to be done." Sinners tested and decided not to approve to retain God in their knowledge; in response, God then gave them over to an unapproved (ἀδόκιμος, adokimos) mind. In 1 Cor 9:27, Paul states, "But I discipline my body and keep it under control, lest after preaching to others I myself should be disqualified (ἀδόκιμος, adokimos)." Is Paul saying that he is exercising self-control to make sure he does not lose his salvation? Or he may be entertaining the possibility that he is a counterfeit or false believer. Or is he talking about being disqualified from his prize (as in a race)? Given how many times Paul shows his confidence about his salvation and being chosen by God as an apostle in his letters, it seems unlikely Paul would

---

78. Oswald, *Lectures on Romans*, 360.
79. Prenter, *Spiritus Creator*, 57.
80. As quoted in Letham, "Saving Faith and Assurance," 36.

entertain the possibility that he may be a counterfeit false believer. So the first or the third option seem more likely here. I believe the third option is the most probable given Paul's expressed belief in the doctrine of election based not on human choice but God's (Rom 8:29, 30, 33; 9:11; 11:7, 28; Eph 1:5, 11). So Paul is saying that he disciplines himself not to be disqualified from the heavenly rewards after encouraging others to exercise self-control to run their races well (1 Cor 9:24–27).

In 2 Tim 3:8, Paul says, "Just as Jannes and Jambres opposed Moses, so these men also oppose the truth, men corrupted in mind and disqualified (ἀδόκιμοι, adokimoi) regarding the faith." Titus 1:16 states, "They profess to know God, but they deny him by their works. They are detestable, disobedient, unfit (ἀδόκιμοι, adokimoi) for any good work." In Heb 6:8, it says, "But if it bears thorns and thistles, it is worthless (ἀδόκιμοι, adokimoi) and near to being cursed, and its end is to be burned." The author of Hebrews is anonymous and most likely not Paul, but his use of *adokimoi* is consistent with Paul's use.

In 2 Cor 13:5–7, our passage in view, the word appears three times (once in each verse), and each time it means "fail to meet the test" or "counterfeit": "unless indeed you fail to meet the test" (or "unless you are counterfeits") in verse 5; "we have not failed the test" (or "we are not counterfeits") in verse 6; and "though we may seem to have failed" (or "though we may seem like counterfeits") in verse 7. Overall, it seems that Paul often uses the word ἀδόκιμοι (*adokimoi*) to refer to those who are disqualified or counterfeit in their faith. That also seems to be the most probable meaning in 2 Cor 13:5 where Paul is telling the Corinthian believers to examine their faith to see if they are in Christ.

A very closely related word is its antonym, δόκιμος (*dokimos*), appearing seven times in the New Testament. In Rom 14:18, 16:10; 2 Cor 10:18; and 2 Tim 2:15, it means "approved." In 1 Cor 11:19, Paul states, "For there must be factions among you in order that those who are genuine (δόκιμοι, *dokimoi*, plural of δόκιμος, *dokimos*) among you may be recognized." It is an interesting statement as it shows Paul expecting a church to have factions because there are genuine believers and false believers in any given church, and they cannot agree on their faith and practices. As Paul says in Rom 8:5–8, those who live according to the flesh (including false believers in the church) set their minds on the things of the flesh, and those who live according to the Spirit set their minds on the things of the Spirit, so they cannot have the same minds.

Finally, Jas 1:12 states, "Blessed is the man who remains steadfast under trial, for when he has stood the test he will receive the crown of life, which God has promised to those who love him." Here the whole phrase "when he has stood the test" is in Greek δόκιμος γενόμενος (*dokimos genomenos*, "when he has become *dokimos*"). Very similar to this is 1 Pet 1:7 where Peter talks about "the tested genuineness of your faith." The words "tested genuineness" are in Greek δοκίμιον (*dokimion*), which is a similar word to *dokimos*, and it can mean "the process or means of determining the genuineness of something" or "genuineness as a result of a test."[81] So *adokimos* and *dokimos* and similar words are used in the New Testament multiple times to distinguish between those who are tested and proven to be either false or genuine disciples.

Paul uses a similar word in 2 Cor 2:9 when he says, "For this is why I wrote, that I might test you and know whether you are obedient in everything." The words "I might test you and know" (ἵνα γνῶ τὴν δοκιμὴν ὑμῶν) literally mean "I might know your δοκιμὴν (*dokimen*)." *Dokimen* is a similar word to *dokimos*, and it means "the experience of going through a test with special reference to the result, standing a test, character."[82] Paul is saying that he wrote the letter to the Corinthians to test or prove the genuineness of their obedience. Though the test in this case is not about the genuineness of their faith but of their obedience, we can see that Paul uses the word group (*dokimos*, *dokimion*, and *dokime*) to refer to the genuineness of something, whether faith or obedience.

It is clear then that the NT authors are thinking about their churches along the lines of mixed communities where there are both genuine and false believers. These false believers do not know they are false believers because they consider themselves genuine believers, and hence they are self-deceived. The challenge of the New Testament authors was that in addition to the Jew-gentile tension in many of their churches, the problems of Judaizers, legalism, antinomianism, factions, persecutions from outside, and the danger of apostasy, they also had to address the issue of the presence of self-deceived false believers. This may have been even more challenging because those who were false believers were not consciously aware of the fact that they were false believers because they were self-deceived.

One approach to deal with this that seems repeated in the New Testament is to issue warnings against being deceived (e.g., Gal 6:3, 7; 1 Cor

---

81. Bauer et al., *Greek-English Lexicon*, s.v. "δοκίμιον," 226.
82. Bauer et al., *Greek-English Lexicon*, s.v. "δοκιμή," 226.

6:9–10; Jas 1:16, 22; 1 John 1:8). For example, Gal 6:7 states, "Do not be deceived: God is not mocked, for whatever one sows, that will he also reap." First Corinthians 6:9-10 states, "Or do you not know that the unrighteous will not inherit the kingdom of God? Do not be deceived: neither the sexually immoral, nor idolaters, nor adulterers, nor men who practice homosexuality, nor thieves, nor the greedy, nor drunkards, nor revilers, nor swindlers will inherit the kingdom of God." Other approaches include emphasizing the need for the fruit (e.g., Matt 3:8, 10; 7:16-20; 12:33; 13:23; 21:43, Mark 4:20; Luke 6:44; 8:14-15; John 15:1-17; Gal 5:22-23; Heb 12:11), manifestations of the Spirit versus flesh (e.g., John 3:6; Rom 8:1-17; Gal 5:16-17; 6:8), and warnings against apostasy (e.g., Matt 13:21; 24:10; Mark 4:17; Luke 8:13; John 16:1; Heb 2:1-3; 3:7—4:13; 6:4-8; 10:26-31; 12:12-18, 25-29). Tragically, many false believers will find out only when they stand before Jesus that they do not really know him (Matt 7:21-23). Helping self-deceived false believers to become genuine regenerate believers should be one of the important tasks for church leaders.

Galatians 6:1–10

Galatians 6:1–10 states:

> Brothers, if anyone is caught in any transgression, you who are spiritual should restore him in a spirit of gentleness. Keep watch on yourself, lest you too be tempted. ² Bear one another's burdens, and so fulfill the law of Christ. ³ For if anyone thinks he is something, when he is nothing, he deceives himself. ⁴ But let each one test his own work, and then his reason to boast will be in himself alone and not in his neighbor. ⁵ For each will have to bear his own load.
> ⁶ Let the one who is taught the word share all good things with the one who teaches. ⁷ Do not be deceived: God is not mocked, for whatever one sows, that will he also reap. ⁸ For the one who sows to his own flesh will from the flesh reap corruption, but the one who sows to the Spirit will from the Spirit reap eternal life. ⁹ And let us not grow weary of doing good, for in due season we will reap, if we do not give up. ¹⁰ So then, as we have opportunity, let us do good to everyone, and especially to those who are of the household of faith.

Galatians shows Paul's thoughts about the existence of false believers in the church through the influence of the Judaizers who were peddling a different gospel. Paul declares that it is those of faith who are the children of Abraham (3:7) and that all who rely on works of the law are under a curse (3:10) and no one is justified before God by the law (3:11). The promised Spirit can only be received through faith (3:14). It is those who were baptized into Christ who have put on Christ (3:27), and they are the children of God, who has sent the Spirit of his Son into their hearts, so they cry, "Abba! Father!" (4:6). They have come to know God and be known by him (4:9). For those who try to keep the Jewish law, Paul is afraid he may have labored in vain (4:10). He is again in the anguish of childbirth until Christ is formed in them (4:19), and he is perplexed about them (4:20). Christ will be of no advantage to those who decide to accept circumcision (5:2), as those who try to be justified by the law are severed from Christ and fallen from grace (5:4). It is those who live by faith through the Spirit who are in Christ Jesus (5:6), and these are led by the Spirit and not under the law (5:18). Those who live by the works of the flesh will not inherit the kingdom of God (5:19–21), but those who belong to Christ have crucified the flesh with its passions and desires (5:24). Those who sow to the flesh will reap corruption (or eternal death), but those who sow to the Spirit will reap eternal life (6:8–9). Circumcision does not count for anything, only a new creation (6:15).

Though it is true that genuine believers also sin and Paul is addressing the whole church, the repeated contrast between those in the flesh and those in the Spirit seems to indicate that Paul is issuing warnings to those in the church but who are not in the Spirit but in the flesh and thus will not inherit eternal life. Commenting on Gal 6:8, Keener mentions, "But one who has only flesh is fully perishable; only those in whose lives the Spirit plays a part have the promise of imperishable, incorruptible, unending life with their creator."[83] Paul is mindful of the false believers in the church, and he wants them to receive the Spirit by faith and not to try to keep the law to attain righteousness in their own efforts manifesting the works of the flesh.

In Gal 6:3 Paul states, "For if anyone thinks he is something, when he is nothing, he deceives himself." Paul issues similar warnings numerous times (e.g., Rom 11:20, 25; 12:3, 16; 1 Cor 8:2). Commenting on this verse, Keener points out that self-deception was a topic of interest and cites Catullus, who complains that someone has deceived himself into thinking that he is a good poet.[84] N. T. Wright comments that self-deception is always a danger when bearing a burden for one another, which he

---

83. Keener, *Galatians*, 553.

84. Keener, *Galatians*, 542. Keener also cites 1 Cor 3:18; Jas 1:23; Jer 37:9 (not LXX); Gal 6:7; 1 Cor 6:9; 15:33.

interprets as straightening out wrong behavior.[85] Thus the guilty party, being self-deceived, does not realize it, and the one who tries to correct the fault is also self-deceived and lacks humility to avoid a sense of superiority.[86] Witherington sees self-deception as a possible reference to those who are not following the pattern of Christ and basing their estimate of self on false criteria.[87] Given Paul's warnings about not inheriting the kingdom in Galatians (e.g., 5:21), the self-deception Paul has in mind here may well include self-deception about one's salvific status.

The context of Gal 6:3 is bearing one another's burdens to fulfill the law of Christ (v. 2), and at the same time bearing one's own load (v. 5) and finding reasons to boast only in comparison with oneself, not with others (v. 4). Self-deception here is again regarding one's self-assessment. When we compare ourselves with others, it aids our self-deception in distorted self-understanding. Different people have different circumstances and opportunities; comparing ourselves with others in less advantageous circumstances will only make us believe we are better than we actually are. Keener comments, "Instead of self-deceptively boasting in ourselves (6:3), we should examine our work and come to a realistic self-appraisal (6:4)."[88]

Then in Gal 6:7, Paul adds, "Do not be deceived: God is not mocked, for whatever one sows, that will he also reap." This is the second warning against self-deception in 6:1–10, indicating Paul's emphasis on its danger. In 6:6–10, the context is Paul's admonition to his readers to continue to do good to one another knowing that they will be rewarded for their good works. The warning is placed in verses 7–8 to those who sow to their flesh as opposed to sowing to the Spirit, the former reaping corruption and the latter eternal life. What is this sowing to the flesh that Paul warns the readers not to be deceived about? In the wider context of Galatians, Paul seems to be referring back to Gal 5:16–24 where he contrasts between the works of the flesh (5:19–21) and the works of the Spirit (5:22–23).[89]

Since the works of the flesh are readily apparent as Paul himself says in 5:19, "Now the works of the flesh are evident," why the need to warn against self-deception in this regard? The answer seems to be in the power of self-deception. Those who are sowing to the flesh and engaged in the works of

---

85. Wright, *Galatians*, 354–55.
86. Wright, *Galatians*, 355.
87. Witherington, *Grace in Galatia*, 426.
88. Keener, *Galatians*, 544.
89. So Bruce, *Epistle to the Galatians*, 265; Moo, *Galatians*, 386.

the flesh can deceive themselves into believing that they are doing important and spiritual works (cf. 6:3). Throughout the letter, Paul strongly rebukes the Galatians' desire to fall into legalism succumbing to the demands of the Judaizers; in 5:13—6:10, he seems to be addressing the opposite error of antinomianism. Self-deception is what enables believers (both genuine and false) to engage in the works of the flesh and still consider themselves important (5:26; 6:3) and their work as spiritual when in fact they may not even attain to eternal life (6:7–8) in the case of the false believers unless they become regenerated.

2 Thessalonians 2:9–12

In 2 Thessalonians, Paul addresses the judgment at Christ's second coming (1:5–12), the man of lawlessness (2:1–12), the need to stand firm (2:13–17), pray (3:1–5), and engage in good works (3:6–15). Second Thessalonians 2:9–12 speaks powerfully about the culpability of those who are self-deceived because they refuse to love the truth and delight in unrighteousness:

> The coming of the lawless one is by the activity of Satan with all power and false signs and wonders, [10] and with all wicked deception for those who are perishing, because they refused to love the truth and so be saved. [11] Therefore God sends them a strong delusion, so that they may believe what is false, [12] in order that all may be condemned who did not believe the truth but had pleasure in unrighteousness.

It is through the activity of Satan that there will be false signs and wonders (v. 9), but those who are duped are culpable in their love of unrighteousness instead of the truth (v. 10). There is a similarity between Paul's description here about Satan's deception of those who refuse to love the truth and the Gen 3 account where the serpent deceives Eve. She ate the forbidden fruit after owning the serpent's deception as her self-deception through her reasoning process ("it was a delight to the eyes") and her desire ("the tree was to be desired to make one wise"), which was an illicit desire since it was desiring what God had prohibited (Gen 2:17; 3:6). In both cases, there is a failure of reason and reflection in their belief in what is false, and this failure is caused by their pleasure in unrighteousness. Again, rational failure stems from moral failure, as we rationalize immoral behavior and engage in our sinful habits after the pattern set by our very first ancestors. When Paul states that as a consequence of their choice to refuse the truth God sends them a strong delusion (2 Thess 2:11), he is making the same point he makes in Rom 11:8 and 10 that even self-deception happens as a result of divine judgment because nothing escapes God's sovereignty. Hiebert notes that God does not send "error" but an inward working of the inevitable consequences of error, so they will fall under the influence of a power working within them: "Since they deliberately chose falsehood in defiance of the truth of God, God subjects them to the power of the error they chose. God uses their choice of evil as the instrument to punish their sin."[90]

In verse 11b, Paul states that the result of God sending them a strong delusion is that they believe what is false. This seems to be referring to the deception of the man of lawlessness:

> The deception of man of sin found a ready response in such men. Their willful rejection of the truth had resulted in the love of evil; evil had become their good. A moral perversion of character had taken place. He who will not accept and obey the truth will inevitably find his delight in unrighteousness.[91]

Hiebert's last sentence makes the same point Isaiah makes in Isa 5:20: "Woe to those who call evil good and good evil." As Paul says in Rom 1:24–25, God gave these people up in the lusts of their hearts because "they exchanged the truth about God for a lie." The reason God sends them a strong delusion is that they have refused to love the truth (2 Thess 2:12). Self-deception is the result of God's judgment in response to people's rejection of the truth, and God's judgment is the outworking of divine justice (2 Thess 1:6). They have become perverted from their true end that, "instead of enjoying God, they enjoy sin. For them evil has become good."[92]

Kim rightly points out that Paul can hardly mean that the true God is the deliberate author of the unbelievers' infatuation with falsehood and wickedness since elsewhere Paul declares that "in their case the god of this world has blinded the minds of the unbelievers, to keep them from seeing the light of the gospel of the glory of Christ, who is the image of God" (2 Cor 4:4).[93] God sending a strong delusion in 2 Thess 2:11 should be understood as God abandoning them to the activity of Satan (v. 9) so that they may be deceived by the man of lawlessness to believe his lies and indulge

90. Hiebert, *1 and 2 Thessalonians*, 344.
91. Hiebert, *1 and 2 Thessalonians*, 345.
92. Morris, *1 and 2 Thessalonians*, 137–38.
93. Kim and Bruce, *1 and 2 Thessalonians*, 611.

in wickedness, incurring condemnation at the final judgment (v. 12).[94] A similar point is made in Rom 1:18–32, but as with Rom 11:7–10, God's sovereign role in judging those who reject his truth is emphasized here. As Morris puts it, "They think that they are acting in defiance of him, but in the end they find that those very acts in which they expressed their defiance were the vehicles of their punishment."[95] This statement eloquently shows the danger of self-deception, especially as it costs the self-deceived their eternal destiny.

In the Pauline Epistles, Paul repeatedly warns against the danger of self-deception because the danger is ever present and the stakes are too high. In Romans, sinners reject God in their self-deceived perception of themselves as being wise (1:21–23). God's judgment comes upon those who engage in self-deception by suppressing the truth (1:18). Some think they are in God's good grace because though they are enslaved to sin, they consider themselves righteous in self-deception (2:17–24). In 1 and 2 Corinthians, Paul rebukes the Corinthians for considering themselves wise (1 Cor 3:18) when they were manifesting spiritual immaturity. Paul issues a dire warning that they will not inherit the kingdom of God if they consistently manifest the works of the flesh (6:9). They should not deceive themselves into believing otherwise. Paul invites them to examine their faith to see if they indeed belong to Christ to make sure that they are not counterfeit Christians (*adokimoi*) (2 Cor 13:5). In Galatians, Paul issues a similar warning against self-deception to those who are manifesting the works of the flesh and thinking that they will inherit eternal life (Gal 6:7–8). In 2 Thessalonians, Paul declares that those who refuse to love the truth are not only deceived by Satan and by themselves but are condemned by God to believe what is false (2:9–12). Self-deception, Satan's deception, and God's judgment are all closely connected.

How can we apply Paul's teachings on self-deception to our lives? First, we need to realize that considering ourselves wise is a clear sign that we are self-deceived. Feeling safe in our salvation while our lives are characterized by sinful patterns is another red flag that should be taken seriously. Catching ourselves dismissing or suppressing what we know to be true lest it jeopardizes our cherished beliefs should send a strong signal that we are guilty of self-deception. Because it is possible to belong to a solidly biblical church and still be self-deceived about our faith and salvation, there should

---

94. Kim and Bruce, *1 and 2 Thessalonians*, 611.
95. Morris, *First and Second Thessalonians*, 235.

be a healthy amount of self-examination (2 Cor 13:5) though too much introspection is not helpful.

HEBREWS AND GENERAL EPISTLES

Hebrews Warning Passages

There is no consensus today on who the author of Hebrews is, though Paul, Barnabas, Apollos, Luke, Priscilla, and others have been proposed as the author. If there is consensus, it is that the author is best left anonymous—we just don't know who the author is. However, there are things we can know about the author from the internal evidence. Priscilla seems to be an unlikely candidate because the author uses a masculine participle when he refers to himself in Heb 11:32: "For time would fail me to tell of (διηγούμενον, *diēgoumenon*)..." If the author was Priscilla, there is no good reason why she would have used a masculine or neuter participle here. To suggest that she did it deliberately to pass herself off as a male to increase the impact of the letter in a male-dominated society may raise the question about the author's integrity and the inspiration of the Scripture. Whether the author was Priscilla or some male pastor, it does not affect the interpretation of the letter. The author was a Jewish minister writing before the fall of Jerusalem in AD 70, probably sometime in the 60s, to mostly Jewish recipients. He was a gifted preacher and knew the recipients well (5:11–14; 10:32–34; 13:18–19, 22–25).

Hebrews was a sermon sent as a letter, and among many reasons for the letter, the author had one urgent need he wanted to address—to prevent the readers' apostasy (falling away from their faith in Christ) as they were experiencing persecutions and contemplating going back to Judaism. He does so by clearly presenting Christ as the divine and eternal new high priest who ushered in the new covenant through his once-for-all sacrifice of himself, making the old covenant with its temple, priesthood, and animal sacrifices obsolete (8:13). It would be utter foolishness to go back to a religious system that cannot save because its function was not to save but to point to Christ. It would make no sense to leave Christ who is the only high priest who can save to the uttermost those who draw near to God through him because he always lives to intercede for them (7:25).

The letter to the Hebrews contains warning passages (2:1–3; 3:7—4:13; 6:4–8; 10:26–31; 12:15–17, 25) that have scholars divided into at least four different camps of interpreting the identity of the apostates and the nature of their judgment. Some believe the warning is only hypothetical, while others believe that the warning is real but what is warned against is not loss of salvation but loss of reward. Among those who believe that the warning is real and the judgment is eternal damnation, the group comprising the majority of scholars, Arminians (those who agree with the theology of Jacob Arminius of the sixteenth century) believe that the warning is addressed to genuine believers who may end up losing their salvation if they apostatize. Calvinists (those who agree with the theology of John Calvin of the sixteenth century), on the other hand, believe that the warning is addressed to those in the church who have not been regenerated, and if they fall away from their professed faith they will forfeit their chance of salvation and be doomed to eternal damnation.

It is highly unlikely any consensus will be achieved any time soon, but the question that is rarely raised in interpreting the warning passages in Hebrews is that of self-deception. How does the factor of self-deception play a role in interpreting the warning passages and the letter as a whole? As we have seen and will see more, self-deception is addressed throughout the Old and the New Testaments. How about Hebrews? Hebrews does mention the deceitfulness of sin (3:13). Could there be self-deceived false believers among the recipients? If this community did not have any false believers, it would be a highly unusual church since Jesus himself had predicted that the believing community would be a mixed community of genuine and false believers.[96] It is much more probable that this church also had false believers, and if that is the case, then the warning passages would at least include them among those who are warned. Stedman concurs: "No matter what careful expedients are employed to make sure that all church members are born again, it is almost certain that there is no congregation which is not just such a mixed multitude as the writer of Hebrews addresses."[97]

Factoring in the self-deceived false believers can shed light on the interpretation of the warning passages. They are addressed as believers as it is their self-perceived identity, and the author as a pastor addresses them as believers, just as pastors in general would address their congregations. Descriptions of their Christian experiences in Heb 6:4–5 ("those who have once been enlightened, who have tasted the heavenly gift, and have shared in the Holy Spirit, and have tasted the goodness of the word of God and the

---

96. See the discussion of Matt 7:21–23 above.
97. Stedman, *Hebrews*, 72.

powers of the age to come") and in 10:29 that they were "sanctified" by the blood of the covenant apply even to the false believers because that is how they view themselves. It is also phenomenologically true—they give every appearance of being genuine believers in the eyes of all members in the community including themselves since only God and no one else can tell what is in human hearts (Jer 17:9).

This helps us understand how the author could address the false believers as if they were genuine believers. His goal is not to accuse them of hypocrisy or to separate between genuine and false believers, because he himself cannot tell them apart with any certainty as long as they maintain their profession of faith. Instead, his intention is to encourage all his readers to persevere through persecution and not to fall away from the Christian community so that they may be saved and enter God's rest (4:10–11). If one takes the Arminian interpretation that the warnings are addressed to the genuine believers, self-deceived false believers can still be included among the addressees. The difference between the two groups would just be that if regenerate believers fall away, they will lose their salvation, and if unregenerate false believers fall away, they will lose the salvation they thought they had and a chance to be saved.

The letter reveals that the author of Hebrews does have two groups of people in mind—genuine and false believers. Believers who can enjoy present confidence of their salvation (6:9–10; 10:39) are consistently distinguished from the individuals in the community who are in danger of eternal judgment (6:4–8; 10:26–31) because of their unbelief due to the repeated hardening of their hearts when they hear God's voice (3:8, 15; 4:7). They have not yet entered God's rest (4:1, 11), and have not obtained the grace of God (12:15). The author makes extensive use of the example of the wilderness generation in his warning toward his readers, which means that he sees a close parallel between the situation of the wilderness generation and that of his readers. Specifically, he seems to see a parallel between the individuals in Moses' congregation to whom Moses' warnings were directed and those in the author's congregation whose hearts remained unchanged. In Heb 12:15 the author warns: "See to it that no one fails to obtain the grace of God; that no 'root of bitterness' springs up and causes trouble, and by it many become defiled." This is a clear reference to Deut 29:18: "Beware lest there be among you a man or woman or clan or tribe whose heart is turning away today from the Lord our God to go and serve the gods of those nations. Beware lest there be among you a root bearing poisonous and bitter fruit."[98] In both cases, even though these individuals are in God's community, their hardening of hearts will result in God's judgment.

What does failing to obtain the grace of God mean? In Heb 12:15, the author links it to a root of bitterness springing up and causing trouble, and in the original context of Deut 29:18–21, it refers to the hardening of one's heart when hearing the words of the covenant (v. 19). In response, God refuses to forgive that person, blotting out his name from under heaven (v. 20), and singling him out from all the tribes of Israel for calamity according to the curses of the Mosaic covenant (v. 21). Failing to obtain the grace of God, then, is to fall under God's wrath due to hardening of the heart. Guthrie sees missing the grace of God as rejecting the gospel and missing the forgiveness offered by Christ's sacrifice.[99]

How does recognizing that false believers are among the congregation help us understand the warning passages better? One of the challenges in interpreting the warning passages is that the apostates to whom the warnings are addressed seem to be described as genuine believers but the consequence of the apostasy seems to be eternal judgment. The author uses "we" to identify himself with those to whom he issues the warnings (2:1, 3; 10:26; 12:25). Is it not a clear indication that the author is saying that anyone, including himself, can fall away? The consequence of falling away seems to be much more than just losing rewards since it will be a worse punishment than death (10:29). There is no more sacrifice for sins remaining (10:26) as a result of trampling underfoot the Son of God and profaning the blood of the covenant (10:29). Interpreting these warnings as simply losing reward does not seem to do justice to the nature of the judgment the author is describing.

For Arminian scholars, the warning passages do not pose any problem because they believe that genuine believers can lose their salvation, as the author of Hebrews places a condition of perseverance for final salvation (e.g., 3:6, 14). However, once we conclude that these warning passages teach that genuine believers can lose their salvation, we run into another challenge from the rest of the letter. The author offers much assurance to the readers about their final salvation, not based on their perseverance but on Christ's work for them. The author of Hebrews presents Jesus as (1) the author and perfecter of their salvation (12:2); (2) the divine-human intercessor (2:18; 4:14–16; 5:2; 7:25); (3) the inaugurator and guarantor of the new covenant (7:22; 8:8–12; 10:14–18); (4) the all-sufficient sacrifice and faithful high

---

98. So Cockerill, *Epistle to the Hebrews*, 636; Guthrie, *Hebrews*, 404.

99. Guthrie, *Hebrews*, 404.

priest (2:17; 9:26–28; 10:14, 23); and (5) the faithful provider of God's rest and his saving grace (4:9–10; 12:23).[100] Let's unpack these points.

Though salvation awaits the future, and believers are to persevere in this life to attain their eschatological salvation, they can nevertheless enjoy the assurance of salvation in the present life. First, Jesus, who is the author and perfecter of their faith (12:2), has gone into the heavenly sanctuary by his own blood, securing their redemption (9:12). Second, he intercedes for them as a perfect intercessor who is both fully divine, able to save to the uttermost those who draw near to God through him (7:25), and fully human who, because he himself suffered when tempted, can help those who are being tempted (2:14–18). Third, he is the inaugurator and guarantor of the new covenant (7:22) that has internalized the law through the Spirit and provided complete forgiveness of sins (8:8–12; 10:15–18). Fourth, Jesus has perfected those who are being sanctified for all time by a single offering (10:14), giving them confidence to enter God's presence (10:19) because Jesus who made the promise is faithful (10:23). Fifth, believers are said to have already entered God's rest in the present (4:9–10), have come to the heavenly Jerusalem (12:22), and have been enrolled in heaven (12:23) even though the final rest remains the future. Finally, the genuine believers who can enjoy present confidence in their salvation (6:9–10; 10:39) are consistently distinguished from the individuals in the community who are in danger of eternal judgment because of their unbelief due to the repeated hardening of their hearts when they hear God's voice (3:8, 15; 4:7). Thus they have not yet entered God's rest (4:1, 11) and have not obtained the grace of God (12:15).

Therefore, genuine believers can enjoy the confidence of their salvation (6:9–10; 10:39). The author does not seem to base their salvation on their ability to persevere but on what Christ has done and is doing for them to guarantee their salvation (6:17; 7:22, 25). But there are those in the congregation who do not get to enjoy such assurance of salvation because they are not yet regenerated, and the new covenant promises of a new heart and forgiveness of sins have not become a reality to them. Neither the author nor the congregation knows exactly who they are because they not only profess faith in Jesus just like the rest of the believers but also have behaved like the rest of them—phenomenologically speaking, that is, as it appears to human eyes. They have not experienced the new covenant reality of a new heart through the indwelling of the Holy Spirit and forgiveness of their sins, and they have been hardening their hearts when they heard God's voice (Heb

---

100. See my article on "Assurance of Salvation" for more details.

3:7, 15; 4:7) to put their trust in Jesus. But much of this is going on at a subconscious level. They do not know in their conscious mind that they do not believe in Jesus just as the wilderness generation did not think that they did not believe in YHWH though it was unbelief that put them in danger of apostasy (3:19, "So we see that they were unable to enter because of unbelief"). Their identity as self-deceived false believers will only be revealed when they fall away from their profession of faith in Jesus and from the believing community and ultimately in the final judgment. The author as their pastor does not want any in his congregation to drift away and fail to inherit such a great salvation (2:3), but only by remaining in the believing community, even in the face of persecution, will they have a chance to inherit it.

Hebrews 3:13

Hebrews 3:13 warns against the deceitfulness of sin: "But exhort one another every day, as long as it is called 'today,' that none of you may be hardened by the deceitfulness of sin." As we have seen, the deceptive nature of sin runs throughout Scripture from the account of the fall (Gen 3:13) to the final days of human history (2 Thess 2:9–10).[101] Sin is intrinsically deceptive as there is always an urge to cover up and obstruct knowledge of itself. That is why darkness is used as a metaphor for the ways of the wicked (e.g., Prov 4:19; Eph 5:8). According to Eph 4:22, our sinful desires are deceitful: "to put off your old self, which belongs to your former manner of life and is corrupt through deceitful desires." Here the "deceitful desires" are sinful desires that are deceitful in that they cover up their sinfulness and put on a presentable front. Unrepentant sinners do not consider their way of life sinful because they desire to indulge in sin but want to consider themselves as decent and moral human beings. Their desires deceive them and make their sins look acceptable and even righteous so they may continue to engage in them even though their sins are leading them to eternal death. Paul adds that in order for them to have true righteousness and holiness, they must be renewed in their minds and put on the new self (Eph 4:24). They must see through the deceitfulness of their sinful desires.

What does the author of Hebrews mean by being "hardened by the deceitfulness of sin"? Throughout the letter, he warns them against apostasy and reverting to Judaism. In the rest of the Scripture, hardening is almost always about the hardening of the heart against God. So also in Hebrews,

---

101. Mounce, *Romans*, 165.

the author seems to be warning against apostasy. The wider context of Heb 3:7—4:13 confirms that the reference is to the hardening of hearts in apostasy like the wilderness generation who perished through their unbelief and rebellion. Sin deceives believers to the point of apostasy if left unchecked. Since the author of Hebrews seems to believe that regenerate believers are those who persevere in their faith through Christ's high priestly intercession for them, among other reasons, it is the self-deceived false believers who are in danger through their sins that can harden them into apostasy.

Against the danger of apostasy through unbelief and the deceitfulness of sin, the preventative measure the author of Hebrews prescribes to the readers is mutual exhortation: "But exhort one another every day, as long as it is called 'today' that none of you may be hardened by the deceitfulness of sin" (3:13). Sin's deception must be countered by perennial dosage of the truth of the word of God through mutual exhortation. The Greek word translated as "exhort" is παρακαλέω (parakaleo), and in Heb 3:13 it means "to urge strongly, appeal to, urge, exhort, encourage."[102] Another meaning of the word, listed in Bauer et al.'s Greek-English dictionary as the first meaning, is "to ask to come and be present" or "to call to one's side." A noun that comes from this verb is παράκλητος (parakletos), and it means "one who appears in another's behalf, mediator, intercessor, helper."[103] This is the word Jesus used to refer to the Holy Spirit when he mentioned that he would send the Spirit to the disciples as "another helper" (ἄλλον παράκλητον, *alon parakletos*) to be with them forever (John 14:16). Jesus calls the Holy Spirit "another" *parakletos* because Jesus himself is also their *parakletos*.

In Heb 3:13, the author desires that the readers should daily encourage one another to stay the course, resisting the temptation of sin's deceitful lures. In that way, each of them can be *parakletos* to one another, providing much-needed help in their faith journeys. Only if they hold their original confidence firm to the end, can they know that they have become sharers (μέτοχοι, *metochoi*) in Christ (3:14). The author uses the word *metochoi* several times in his letter: "*companions*" (1:9), "*sharers* of a heavenly calling" (3:1), "*sharers* of the Holy Spirit" (6:4), "If you are left without discipline, in which all have become *sharers*, then you are illegitimate children and not sons" (12:8) (translations mine). The idea is that of participation or involvement. So when the author says in 3:14 that perseverance is a necessary condition for having become a sharer in Christ, he is saying that

---

102 Bauer et al., *Greek-English Lexicon*, s.v. "παρακαλέω," 765.
103 Bauer et al., *Greek-English Lexicon*, s.v. "παράκλητος," 766.

without perseverance, one cannot have become the sharer in Christ—there is no salvation.

A question may arise: How can perseverance, the successful outcome of which awaits the future, be a condition of a past reality of having become a sharer in Christ? The author uses the verb γεγόναμεν (*genonamen*, "we have become"), a pluperfect tense form of the verb γίνομαι (*ginomai*, "become"), when he says "we have become sharers in Christ." The answer is that this condition is not a cause-effect condition but an evidence-inference condition. Perseverance is not the cause of having become a sharer in Christ but the evidence of it.[104] The author uses a very similar evidence-inference condition in 3:6: "But Christ is faithful over God's house as a son. And we are his house, if indeed we hold fast our confidence and our boasting in our hope." Perseverance in our faith in Christ is the evidence that we are now God's house.

Hebrews 4:1–11

Hebrews 4:1–11 states:

> Therefore, while the promise of entering his rest still stands, let us fear lest any of you should seem to have failed to reach it. ² For good news came to us just as to them, but the message they heard did not benefit them, because they were not united by faith with those who listened. ³ For we who have believed enter that rest, as he has said,
> "As I swore in my wrath,
> 'They shall not enter my rest,'"
> although his works were finished from the foundation of the world. ⁴ For he has somewhere spoken of the seventh day in this way: "And God rested on the seventh day from all his works."
> ⁵ And again in this passage he said,
> "They shall not enter my rest."
> ⁶ Since therefore it remains for some to enter it, and those who formerly received the good news failed to enter because of disobedience, ⁷ again he appoints a certain day, "Today," saying through David so long afterward, in the words already quoted,
> "Today, if you hear his voice,
> do not harden your hearts."

---

104. Cf. Wallace, *Greek Grammar*, 683.

> ⁸ For if Joshua had given them rest, God would not have spoken of another day later on. ⁹ So then, there remains a Sabbath rest for the people of God, ¹⁰ for whoever has entered God's rest has also rested from his works as God did from his.
> ¹¹ Let us therefore strive to enter that rest, so that no one may fall by the same sort of disobedience.

In 4:1 where the author says, "Therefore, while the promise of entering his rest still stands, let us fear lest any of you should seem to have failed to reach it," he is warning that there may be individuals who have failed to enter God's rest. This rest is a metaphor for salvation experience in the context of 4:1–11 since it is connected with the gospel message and believing (v. 2, "For good news came to us just as to them, but the message they heard did not benefit them, because they were not united by faith with those who listened").[105] Then in verse 3, the author contrasts those who have not believed with others who have: "For we who have believed enter that rest."[106]

Both the wilderness generation and the readers were faced with formidable foes: for the former, the foes were the inhabitants of Canaan against whom the Israelites felt like grasshoppers (Num 13:33), and for the latter, the foes are intimidating persecutions they have previously experienced (10:32–34) and will continue to face. In both cases, there are two groups who respond differently: those who respond in faith (like Joshua and Caleb) and the others who respond in unbelief (like the rest of the wilderness generation). Jude declares that the wilderness generation was destroyed because of their unbelief: "Now I want to remind you, although you once fully knew it, that Jesus, who saved a people out of the land of Egypt, afterward destroyed those who did not believe" (Jude 5). That is why the author of Hebrews spends much time comparing his readers with the wilderness generation and warns them against unbelief (3:7—4:13). As F. F. Bruce observed, "they too had experienced the redeeming power of God; they too had the promise of the homeland of the faithful to look forward to; but one thing could prevent them from realizing that promise, just as it had prevented the mass of the Israelites who left Egypt from entering Canaan—and that one thing was unbelief."[107] Unbelief was what ultimately

---

105. See Attridge, *Hebrews*, 126–28, for the connection between the concept of rest and soteriological motifs in Hebrews.

106. Fanning, "Classical Reformed View," 196. Fanning remarks, "The verse does not seem to allow for the possibility that those who begin in faith may in the end actually fail to enter."

107. Bruce, *Epistle to the Hebrews*, 69.

caused the wilderness generation to fail to enter the promised land, and it is what was preventing the self-deceived false believers among the readers from receiving their salvation.

What separated the self-deceived false believers from the genuine believers? What prevented them from attaining their salvation? Once again, the heart seems to be the issue. The author pleads with the readers not to harden their hearts when they hear God's voice (e.g., 3:15; 4:7). The false believers have not experienced the new covenant blessing of a new heart. New covenant fulfillment is the defining characteristic of the Christian community, and it results in a change of heart. The new covenant is such an important theme in the letter to the Hebrews, and it is the letter's governing narrative.[108] One of the key features of the new covenant is that God's laws will be written in the hearts of his people. In 8:10 (and similarly in 10:16) the author quotes Jer 31:33: "For this is the covenant that I will make with the house of Israel after those days, declares the Lord: I will put my law within them, and I will write it on their hearts. And I will be their God, and they shall be my people."

For the author of Hebrews, *heart* is a very important word, appearing no less than eleven times in the letter (3:8, 10, 12, 15; 4:7, 12; 8:10; 10:16, 22 [twice]; 13:9). Three times, he warns the readers against hardening their hearts, quoting Ps 95:7–8 twice (3:8, 15; 4:7). Twice, he talks about a heart that goes astray or does not believe (3:10, 12). Once he says that the word of God discerns the thoughts and intentions of the heart (4:12). He seems to be saying that they may be able to deceive others and even themselves but not God, since God knows their hearts. Twice the author talks about the new covenant written in the hearts of God's people (8:10; 10:16), both times quoting Jer 31:33. Three times he talks about desirable conditions of the heart: having full assurance of faith (10:22), being cleansed from evil conscience (10:22), and being strengthened by grace (13:9).

The author of Hebrews is in good company when he makes the heart a central issue that determines one's covenant relationship with God. After forty years of leading the exodus generation in the wilderness, Moses attributed his congregation's failure to obey God to the condition of their hearts:

> You have seen all that the Lord did before your eyes in the land of Egypt, to Pharaoh and to all his servants and to all his land, the great trials that your eyes saw, the signs, and those great wonders.

---

108. Lehne, *New Covenant in Hebrews*; Allen, "Forgotten Spirit," 65.

> But to this day the Lord has not given you a heart to understand or eyes to see or ears to hear. (Deut 29:2b–4)

Moses knew the reason the people continued in their rebellion and unbelief after forty years of God's miraculous provision for them was that their hearts had remained unchanged. He also knew that because of this, they would experience God's curses contained in the covenant:

> 24 all the nations will say, "Why has the Lord done thus to this land? What caused the heat of this great anger?" 25 Then people will say, "It is because they abandoned the covenant of the Lord, the God of their fathers, which he made with them when he brought them out of the land of Egypt, 26 and went and served other gods and worshiped them, gods whom they had not known and whom he had not allotted to them. 27 Therefore the anger of the Lord was kindled against this land, bringing upon it all the curses written in this book, 28 and the Lord uprooted them from their land in anger and fury and great wrath, and cast them into another land, as they are this day." (Deut 29:24-28)

For Moses as well as Jeremiah, for God's people to experience covenant blessings from God, they needed to hear and obey God's voice with their whole hearts.[109] People's hearts turning away is equated to not hearing God's voice, and the consequence is perishing (Deut 30:17–18a, "But if your heart turns away, and you will not hear, but are drawn away to worship other gods and serve them, I declare to you today, that you shall surely perish"). In order for them to live, they had to love YHWH, obey his voice, and hold fast to him (30:20). This is why there is a repeated command in Hebrews not to harden their hearts when they hear God's voice (Heb 3:8, 13, 15; 4:7). In the context of the wilderness generation that the author of Hebrews refers to, hardening of heart seems to refer to refusing to believe

---

109. See Deut 30:1–3, 9–10. When Moses' prophetic pronouncement about the future exile (Deut 30:1) was fulfilled and the people of Judah were about to be taken into exile by the Babylonians, Jeremiah also made a prophetic statement concerning them that sounded very much like that of Moses: "I will give them a heart to know that I am the Lord, and they shall be my people and I will be their God, for they shall return to me with their whole heart" (Jer 24:7). Then Jeremiah later sent a letter to the exiled people to whom he prophesied again: "you will seek me and find me when you seek me with all your heart" (29:13). Then YHWH would bring them back to their homeland from the place of exile, just as Moses had said.

in God (Num 14:1–11).[110] Hardening of heart is a response of unbelief to God's voice in apostasy.

According to Jeremiah, what was needed for God's people to hear and obey God's voice with their whole hearts was to circumcise and to remove the foreskin of their hearts: "Circumcise yourselves to the Lord; remove the foreskin of your hearts, O men of Judah and inhabitants of Jerusalem; lest my wrath go forth like fire, and burn with none to quench it, because of the evil of your deeds" (Jer 4:4). Moses also had prophesied that future generations would experience God's deliverance through a change of their heart: "And the Lord your God will circumcise your heart and the heart of your offspring, so that you will love the Lord your God with all your heart and with all your soul, that you may live" (Deut 30:6). A call for repentance had been issued: "Wash your heart from evil, that you may be saved" (Jer 4:14); however, a stubborn and rebellious heart turns aside from God because there is no fear of God (5:23–24). They refused to take correction and refused to repent even after God consumed them (5:3). God will not pardon them (5:7) because they have eyes that do not see and ears that do not hear, and they do not fear God (5:21–22). They resist God because "their hearts are uncircumcised" (6:10).

The circumcision imagery is significant since circumcision was the obligation that Abraham and his descendants were to fulfill in the Abrahamic covenant (Gen 17:10–14). Circumcision was to be a sign of the covenant between God and Abraham and his descendants, and the covenant was to be an everlasting covenant in their flesh through circumcision (vv. 11, 13). Anyone who was not circumcised was to be cut off from God's people because he had broken God's covenant (v. 14). So Jeremiah's application of the circumcision imagery to the idea of the heart indicates that, to Jeremiah, circumcision is the sign of God's covenant with his people under the new covenant also—but this time circumcision is to be not in the flesh but in the heart. Just as anyone who was not circumcised in the flesh was to be cut off from God's people under the old covenant, anyone under the new covenant who was not circumcised in the heart would also be cut off from God's people. The New Testament language of the circumcision of the heart is regeneration.

Time and again, the heart is the issue for Jeremiah. There must be a change of heart for the people of God to return to God and be saved. Otherwise, only God's fierce wrath and his judgment are to be expected.

---

110. Lane, *Hebrews*, 64.

Jeremiah repeats three times this exact sentence: "Shall I not punish them for these things? declares the Lord; and shall I not avenge myself on a nation such as this?" (5:9, 29; 9:9). These words of Jeremiah find their parallel in the warning passages in Hebrews where God's severe judgment is pronounced upon the apostates who have unbelieving hearts: just because one belongs to a church does not guarantee that they have become God's children. Those who do not subject themselves to God's discipline are illegitimate children—they do not belong to God (Heb 12:8).[111] So the author is distinguishing those individuals who harden their hearts when they hear God's voice, resulting in unbelief and disobedience, from those in whom God's new covenant promise of a new heart has been fulfilled because the good news they heard was united with faith.[112] The former of these two groups are the self-deceived false believers.

The author of Hebrews as a pastor is trying his best to keep them from falling away from Christ and the believing community by warning them about the eternal judgment on the apostates and painting the picture of the incomparable superiority of the new covenant to the old covenant in all aspects including the high priest, sacrifice, temple, and the final outcome. The old covenant had the human, sinful, and short-lived priests, but the new covenant has the divine, sinless, and eternal high priest. The old covenant had animal sacrifices that could only provide ritual and external purifications, but the new covenant has the perfect and once-for-all sacrifice of Christ that provides internal and complete cleansing from sins. The old covenant had the tabernacle and the temple that were mere copies of the heavenly sanctuary of the new covenant. The old covenant was designed to be a foreshadow of the real thing to come—the reality of the new covenant that has fulfilled and replaced the old covenant. By not hardening their hearts when they hear God's voice can the self-deceived false believers experience the new covenant reality of the circumcised hearts and regeneration that can prevent their apostasy.

---

111. As Rodriguez points out, Jesus shapes the lives of those who belong to the truth ("Church: Sign and First Fruit," 273).

112. Heb 4:2: "For good news came to us just as to them, but the message they heard did not benefit them, because they were not united by faith with those who listened."

What the Bible Says about the Dangers of Self-Deception

James 1:22

James, the author of the letter of James, was a half-brother of Jesus, and he was not a believer until he met the risen Jesus, after which he became a leader in the church of Jerusalem (John 7:5; 1 Cor 15:7; Gal 2:9). The Epistle of James is considered by many as the earliest New Testament book, written in the 40s before the Jerusalem Council was held in AD 49. A few reasons for such an early dating are that James addresses the Jewish audience (1:1) who were still meeting in synagogues for their worship (2:2), and there is no hint of Jew/gentile conflict in the letter, indicating that gentile mission had not been initiated at the time James wrote his letter. Most, if not all, of James's readers were Jewish believers.

Many echoes of Jesus' teachings are found in James. Some examples are topics such as favoritism (2:1–13; cf. Matt 5:46–48), the golden rule (2:8; cf. Mark 12:31; Matt 22:39; Luke 10:27), genuine faith (2:14–26; cf. Matt 7:15–27), the tongue (3:1–12; cf. Luke 6:43–45), true versus false wisdom (3:3–18; cf. Matt 11:19), a divided heart (4:5–8; cf. Matt 6:24), condemning others (4:11–12; cf. Matt 7:1–5), wealth (4:13–17; cf. Matt 6:28–34), endurance (5:7–11; Matt 24:13), oaths (5:12; Matt 5:33–37), and prayers (5:13–18; cf. Matt 21:21–22). Though James was not converted until after Jesus' post-resurrection appearance to him, it is not hard to see that Jesus must have had a deep influence on James during about thirty years of their sibling interactions.

In Jas 2:14–26, James warns against the nominal faith of those who claim to have faith but without substance just as Jesus had similarly warned the religious leaders, and James repeatedly warns against self-deception in his letter (e.g., 1:16, 22, 26). James 1:22 says, "Do not merely listen to the word, and so deceive yourselves. Do what it says." Those who fail to do the word, who are hearers only, are guilty of a dangerous self-deception. The word for "deceive" here is παραλογίζομαι (*paralogizomai*), and it means "deceive, delude, defraud."[113] Being a hearer only and not a doer leads a person to false self-reckoning.[114] Just as we are self-deceived if we are wise in our own eyes when in fact we are not (Prov 26:12), we are self-deceived if we think we are right with God when we are only hearers of the word and not doers (cf. Rom 2:13).

---

113. Bauer et al., *Greek-English Lexicon*, s.v. "παραλογίζομαι," 768.
114. McCartney, *James*, 120.

James 1:22 is a thesis statement of the letter, and the remainder of the letter is the exploration and application of this thesis.[115] This statement is a warning against self-deception of a hearer of the word and not a doer, of having a religion that is empty and foolish.[116] The central theme of the letter of James is the need for genuine faith that manifests itself in life.[117] James's purpose is to urge his readers to test their faith by the criterion that faith without works is useless (2:20), and he provides a series of tests for the readers to determine the genuineness of their faith.[118] "'The testing of your faith' (1:3) seems to be the key which James left hanging at the front door, intended to unlock the contents of the book."[119]

Because embracing the gospel means accepting both its saving power and its call to obedience, James says that people who only hear the word are deceiving themselves. As Moo points out, "They think they have a relationship with God because they regularly attend church, go to Bible studies or read the Bible. But if their listening is not accompanied by obedience, their true situation before God is far different."[120] To hear without doing is to be guilty of self-deception. But what gives rise to self-deception? Why be a hearer but not a doer of the word? For James, it is a consequence of ἐπιθυμία (*epithymia*, "desire") (1:14), which turns back the hearer from the word of God to the desires of self. It is through desire that humans lead themselves astray. "Bound up with this is the human inclination to justify even the most inhuman and reprehensible behaviors when such seem necessary for the fulfillment of our desires."[121] Painter points out the close connection between self-deception and desire/lust. Human desire and lust

---

115. Brosend, *James and Jude*, 51.

116. Brosend, *James and Jude*, 51.

117. Hiebert, "Unifying Theme of James," 223. Hiebert cites other scholars such as McNeile and Lenski approvingly as they make this argument.

118. Hiebert, "Unifying Theme of James," 223.

119. Hiebert, "Unifying Theme of James," 223. Hiebert also affirms that "*tests of living faith* is indeed the unifying theme of the epistle and . . . provides ready access to its contents" ("Unifying Theme of James," 224). Faith is tested by its response to the Word of God (1:19–27), its reaction to partiality (2:1–13), its production of works (2:14–26), its production of self-control through controlling the tongue (3:1–18), its reactions to worldliness (4:1–5:12), and its resort to prayer (5:13–18) ("Unifying Theme of James," 225–31).

120. Moo, *James*, 82; Calvin *Institutes* 1.6.1.

121. Painter, *James*, 79.

cause deceptive rationalization.¹²² Desire played a key role in Eve's decision to eat the forbidden fruit, the very first sin of humanity.

To hear and not to practice is to deceive oneself (Jas 1:22, "But be doers of the word, and not hearers only, deceiving yourselves"), and the context indicates that the self-deception here is about one's salvation, as it best fits with what 1:21b means by receiving the word ("receive with meekness the implanted word, which is able to save your souls"). Receiving the word means not simply to hear but to do, and anyone thinking it to be less than that deceives himself that he has received the word.¹²³

Moo argues that in 1:22 James is showing his dependence on Jesus' teaching (e.g., Luke 11:28: "Blessed rather are those who hear the word of God and obey it").¹²⁴ No one emphasized as strongly as Jesus the need for people touched by God's grace to respond with a radical, world-renouncing obedience.¹²⁵ When James says that people who merely listen to the word deceive themselves, the same verb for "deceive" (παραλογίζομαι, *paralogizomai*) is used by Paul in Col 2:4 about false teachers who deceive people by fine-sounding arguments. In both of these contexts, the idea of "deceive" clearly conveys the meaning of being blinded to the reality of one's true religious state: thinking that they are right with God when they really are not.¹²⁶ Moo declares that those who hear the word and attend church, go to a seminary, or even teach as seminary professors but do not "do" it are all included in this group and are mistaken when they think they are right with God. God's word cannot be divided, and those who fail to do the word, even if they want the benefits of its saving power, have not truly accepted God's word at all.¹²⁷ Davids concurs that those who think that receiving the word means less than hearing the word and doing it deceive themselves

---

122. Painter, *James*, 79: "James here reveals the complexity of self-deception as involving a self-justifying rationale that may be believed and used in argument. The use of *paralogizomenoi heautous* in 1:22 to describe this self-deception, rather than one of the other terms used to speak of being led astray in 1:16 (*me planasthe*) and 1:26 (*apaton*), may imply this deceptive rationalization. The self deceives the self! Compare the use of *heautous planomen* in 1 John 1:8. There are strong theological connections between James and 1 John, and the critique of desire/lust (*epithymia*) in 1 John 2:16–17 is related to the critique in James 1:14–15, but 1 John does not go as far as James in rooting the power of temptation in *epithymia*."

123. Davids, *Commentary on James*, 97; Moo, *Letter of James*, 90.

124. Moo, *Letter of James*, 89.

125. Moo, *Letter of James*, 89.

126. Moo, *Letter of James*, 90.

127. Moo, *Letter of James*, 90.

when they think they received the word—they are self-deceived about their salvation.[128]

Stulac supports this view based on James's own choice of analogy in 1:23–24.[129] The analogy's point is that just as a man sees his reflection in the mirror and goes away without seeing any need to change anything, so is the hearer of the word who does not do what it says. James is warning the readers not to be self-deceived about their very salvation.[130] To persist in sin that kills (1:15) and claim salvation from death is self-contradictory and the practice of self-deception.[131]

James 1:26

The word of God is the means of regeneration in James ("he brought us forth by the word of truth" in 1:18), but hearing the word must be followed by obedience to the word (1:22–27); otherwise, the hearing is useless (1:22–25). True obedience to the word must reveal itself in the power to control the tongue (1:26) and beneficial social activities and personal purity (1:27).[132] James 1:26 states, "If anyone thinks he is religious and does not bridle his tongue but deceives his heart, this person's religion is worthless." Failure to bridle the tongue marks an empty claim to be religious. James's command to be "slow to speak," which is a corollary of "quick to hear" in 1:19, implies controlling the tongue. In 1:26, James is saying that the inability to do this indicates that any claim for spirituality is merely self-deception. Jesus made speech a manifestation of the heart: "The good person out of the good treasure of his heart produces good, and the evil person out of his evil treasure produces evil, for out of the abundance of the heart his mouth speaks" (Luke 6:45).

Speech should arise as a response after listening to God and the neighbor and not as an expression of desire (ἐπιθυμία, *epithymia*) that leads to temptation (1:14, "But each person is tempted when he is lured and enticed by his own desire"). For James, desire leads first to temptation, then to sin, and, ultimately, to death (1:15). Obviously, James is referring to sinful desires of the flesh, not good and healthy desires prompted by the Spirit.

128. Davids, *Commentary on James*, 97.
129. Stulac, *James*, 74.
130. Stulac, *James*, 75.
131. Stulac, *James*, 75.
132. Hiebert, "Unifying Theme of James," 225.

Those who fail to control their tongue deceive their hearts and are not pure in heart (cf. Jas 4:8). An unbridled tongue can deceive the tongue's owner, and just as one is responsible for failing to control the tongue, one is also responsible for deceiving oneself.[133] *Epithymia* (desire) corrupts the heart or is the expression of a corrupt heart, which is pure only when devoted to God and the neighbor. Those who deceive their heart deceive themselves, and reference to the heart signifies corruption at the very core being.[134] As Jer 17:9 declares, "The heart is deceitful above all things, and desperately sick; who can understand it?"

James says that all stumble in many ways, including our speech (3:2), and no human being can tame the tongue. It is a restless evil, full of deadly poison (3:8). Then who can tame it? Only God can. Thus, speech under control is a sign of God's Spirit present and active in a person's life and manifestation of regeneration by the word of truth (1:18). This person has received with meekness the implanted word, which was able to save his soul (1:21). Such regeneration is God's gift coming from above (1:17).

James 2:14–26

In 2:14–26, James delineates what genuine saving faith looks like. Those who think that they have faith in Jesus but their faith falls short of the saving faith would be self-deceived false believers. James compares the faith of someone who claims to have faith, but does not have works to show it, to an empty verbal generosity toward a cold and hungry person without actually giving any food or clothing—it is useless and cannot save the person who possesses it. Here is the passage:

> [14] What good is it, my brothers, if someone says he has faith but does not have works? Can that faith save him? [15] If a brother or sister is poorly clothed and lacking in daily food, [16] and one of you says to them, "Go in peace, be warmed and filled," without giving them the things needed for the body, what good is that? [17] So also faith by itself, if it does not have works, is dead.
> [18] But someone will say, "You have faith and I have works." Show me your faith apart from your works, and I will show you my faith by my works. [19] You believe that God is one; you do well. Even the demons believe—and shudder! [20] Do you want to be shown, you

---

133. McCartney, *James*, 128.
134. Painter, *James*, 81.

foolish person, that faith apart from works is useless? [21] Was not Abraham our father justified by works when he offered up his son Isaac on the altar? [22] You see that faith was active along with his works, and faith was completed by his works; [23] and the Scripture was fulfilled that says, "Abraham believed God, and it was counted to him as righteousness"—and he was called a friend of God. [24] You see that a person is justified by works and not by faith alone. [25] And in the same way was not also Rahab the prostitute justified by works when she received the messengers and sent them out by another way? [26] For as the body apart from the spirit is dead, so also faith apart from works is dead.

James writes this section in an argumentative style called diatribe by which he introduces an interlocutor (objector) who states his own viewpoint as a foil for James's argument (v. 18). By doing so, James takes on those who hold the teaching he combats as if they were present (e.g., "you foolish man" in v. 20) and appeals to his readers to judge the cogency of what he is saying ("you see" in vv. 22, 24).[135] This style strongly suggests that James is combating some false teachers who were setting forth an incorrect view of faith.[136] The interlocutor's viewpoint is that faith can exist apart from works (v. 18). James responds by saying that such faith can be compared to the faith of demons who do believe in God even to the point of a shudder (vv. 18b–19). Obviously, it cannot save its possessors, humans and demons alike, and as demonstrated in the cases of Abraham and Rahab, faith needs to be manifested through works (vv. 20–26). Especially in the case of Rahab, her profession of faith in God would not have saved her from death apart from her works in risking her life to hide the Israelite spies. To have a deficient faith (being a hearer only) and think it will provide salvation would be dangerous self-deception that will cost its possessor eternal destiny, and James wants to prevent that for his readers.

Zane Hodges holds that this passage is dealing with a genuine believer who has "dead faith," which is also genuine faith that saves a person from eternal damnation but not from life's difficulties, and salvation in this passage refers to deliverance from danger, loss, or physical death, not eschatological salvation.[137] Hodges points out that James is addressing them as brothers (v. 14) and thus he must have genuine believers in mind.[138] But

135. Moo, *James*, 99.
136. Moo, *James*, 99.
137. Hodges, *Dead Faith*, 8–15.
138. Hodges, *Dead Faith*, 10.

James addressing the readers as brothers and holding that those who do not have works have deficient faith that cannot save are not incompatible propositions. Pastors would not refrain from addressing their congregations as brothers and sisters just because of the presence of some who are not born again. More importantly, James does not address the person who does not have works (the outworkings or fruit of saving faith) in 2:14–26 as a brother and does not even grant that his claim to have faith is valid ("if someone says he has faith" in v. 14). The point of the passage is that "we are saved through genuine, as opposed to counterfeit, faith."[139]

Hodges's contention that James's use of the expression "dead faith" indicates that he considers this faith as once alive is also without textual support. James compares "dead faith" to the faith of demons (v. 19) since in both cases, the supposed faith cannot save its possessor from eternal damnation (v. 14). James provides examples of Abraham's and Rahab's faith to demonstrate that only when faith is accompanied by works can it justify its possessor, since apart from works, faith is useless and dead (vv. 20–26). Hodges's argument that James is not talking about salvation from eternal condemnation but salvation from physical death in his letter does not find support in the passage and James's letter as a whole. Except for 5:15 where "save" means "to make well," when James uses the word σώζω ($sozo$, "save"), it always denotes deliverance from the final judgment, not salvation from physical death (1:21; 4:12; 5:20). In the rest of the New Testament, the words *save* and *salvation* predominantly denote deliverance from eternal judgment (e.g., Matt 10:28; 16:25; Mark 8:35; Luke 9:24; John 12:25; 1 Pet 1:9). In 2:14 also where James says, "Can that faith save him?" it is referring to the eschatological salvation or the deliverance from the final judgment since James mentions the eschatological judgment in the immediately preceding verses (vv. 12–13). In his letter, James contrasts genuine faith with the false faith of a self-deceived person (1:22, 26) and warns against an appearance of religion without reality. In 2:14–26, James is specifically articulating that any claim to have faith without the outworkings of saving faith cannot save its possessor from eternal judgment. It would be tragic self-deception to believe that such faith can save.[140]

---

139. Cranfield, "Message of James," 338.

140. For a detailed refutation of Hodges's interpretation of Jas 2:14–26, see Pak, "Study of Selected Passages," 220–58.

1 John 1:8

Apostle John, the author of the Johannine literature (Gospel of John, 1–3 John, and Revelation), wrote 1 John around AD 90–95 after he wrote the Gospel.[141] One of the greatest concerns of John in writing 1 John was the issue of false believers in the church. They arose from within the ranks of the church but left the church (2:18–19). To protect his congregation against these false believers, whom he calls the antichrists (2:18) because they deny the true Christ and promote a false one (2:22–23), John provides many tests in the letter by which his readers can discern genuine faith from false faith. These tests include confession that Jesus is the Messiah or the Christ (2:22–23; 4:2–3; 5:5), obedience to Christ's commands (2:3–6; 3:4–10), and love for other believers (2:9–11; 3:10–20; 4:7–11).

In 1 John 1:8, John states, "If we claim to be without sin, we deceive ourselves and the truth is not in us." Here, self-deception is regarding sin when one considers oneself sinless, a case of the failure of self-knowledge. First John reveals that the false believers (often called secessionists by scholars because they seceded from, or left, John's church) considered themselves sinless because they seemed to have bought into an incipient form of Gnosticism or Cerinthianism, Christological heresies that arose in the first century AD that denied Christ's humanity. Cerinthus believed that Christ, who is a spirit from God, came upon human Jesus at baptism but left him before Jesus' death.

According to Irenaeus, a church father and bishop of Lyon in the second century AD:

> [Cerinthus] represented Jesus as having not been born of a virgin, but as being the son of Joseph and Mary according to the ordinary course of human generation, while he nevertheless was more righteous, prudent and wise than other men. Moreover, after his baptism, Christ descended upon him in the form of a dove from the Supreme Ruler, and that then he proclaimed the unknown Father, and performed miracles. But at last Christ departed from Jesus, and that then Jesus suffered and rose again, while Christ remained impassible, inasmuch as he was a spiritual being.[142]

Cerinthus believed that Christ did not become flesh, but only came upon a human Jesus and used him before his death. Thus he denied the doctrine

---

141. See the discussion on the authorship of Johannine literature in John 8:33 above.
142. Irenaeus, *Against Heresies*, 1.26.1.

of incarnation. The secessionists who left John's church either agreed with Cerinthus or believed that Christ only appeared to be human (a heresy called Docetism). Either way, they denied the incarnation of Christ—God the Son taking on humanity (2 John 1:7, "For many deceivers have gone out into the world, those who do not confess the coming of Jesus Christ in the flesh. Such a one is the deceiver and the antichrist"). This denial of the humanity of Christ by distinguishing Christ from the human Jesus led the false believers to reject the significance of what they do with their bodies. They considered what one does with the body as irrelevant since the only thing that mattered was the spirit. This is how they could consider themselves sinless while practicing sin (1:8, 10; 3:4–10). When they left John's church, they formed their own church that taught docetic Christ (Christ who appeared to be human but was only divine and did not die on the cross since God cannot die).[143] They were examples of self-deceived false believers, and John warns his readers against the false teachers who were trying to convert John's congregation to their faulty Christology.

First John is a good example of the danger self-deception poses to the church. The secessionists were so convinced they were genuine believers and their view of Christ was the correct one that they left John's church and formed their own and were actively promoting their false gospel to try to win the people in the Johannine community over to their own (1 John 2:26; 4:1; 2 John 10). The fact that John had to write to warn against these false believers shows that self-deception is dangerous not only to the self-deceived but to all who fall under their influence.

In Hebrews and General Epistles, we see there are similar warnings against self-deception as we find in the rest of the New Testament. In some ways, those warnings are more explicit (e.g., Hebrews warning passages) perhaps because the danger of apostasy is greater due to more persecution (Hebrews), oppression (James), or heretical Christology (1 John). Perseverance in orthodoxy (sound doctrine) with a believing community through trials and hardships is not only a sign of genuine faith but also a means to overcome self-deception and acquire genuine faith.

---

143. Docetism is another related Christological heresy and derives its name from the Greek word δοκέω (*dokeo*), which means "appear, seem." That is, Christ only appeared to be human.

5

So What?

WE HAVE EXAMINED MANY Bible passages that talk about self-deception. Important questions to ask now would be: So what? How does the scriptural teaching on self-deception affect our lives now? What applications can we draw from it? I added applicational thoughts to our discussion of some of the passages and at the end of each of the six sections in chapters 3 and 4 (Pentateuch, Poetical Literature, Prophetic Literature, Gospels and Acts, Pauline Epistles, and Hebrews and General Epistles), and they will be expanded here. And there are some other applicational ideas we have not yet considered.

BENEFITS OF SELF-DECEPTION

Many of the passages we have discussed warn about the dangers of self-deception. Are there any benefits to self-deception? As I cited in the introduction, Ten Elshof notes that self-deception has been called upon to explain irrationality and dysfunction.[1] But he goes on to mention, "Interestingly, it has also been called upon to explain survival and success in a variety of contexts."[2] One of the benefits of self-deception is that it may help survival—to have hope no matter how improbable a situation is (e.g., in the case of terminally ill cancer patients) could potentially increase the chance

---

1. Ten Elshof, *I Told Me So*, 5.
2. Ten Elshof, *I Told Me So*, 5.

What the Bible Says about the Dangers of Self-Deception

of healing.[3] It is also conceivable that a person who is self-deceived in believing that he is more intelligent, charming, and better looking than he really is could experience some positive effects on his professional and personal life.[4] Some empirical research has purported to have shown such positive effects that self-deception has on one's quality of life.[5] In addition, by learning and utilizing mechanisms of self-deception, we can gain empathy with those who have distorted perspectives to help us better understand how they think. These mechanisms could help people survive when going through circumstances that are overwhelming and crippling because self-deception is often a defense mechanism and a subconscious effort to avoid pain and anxiety by filtering out painful information.[6] If we find ourselves in those circumstances, before we gain freedom from self-deception, we need to become capable of handling the truth through the empowerment of the Holy Spirit. Being faced with the truth about ourselves and our circumstances before such empowerment can potentially be debilitating and destructive.

My father passed away from pancreatic cancer when he was only fifty-six years old and my mother fifty-three. He was a very healthy man until he was diagnosed with stage 4 pancreatic cancer about nine months before his death. My mother was not ready for his death because she was very much dependent on him for her livelihood and virtually everything else. She never once believed that he would not recover from his cancer. She was convinced that God would heal him—at least in her conscious mind—and she refused to look into what she may have truly believed deep in her heart because she simply could not bear the thought of him dying. For the nine months of hospitalization, my mother always slept in the same hospital room with my father and always went to dawn prayer meetings to ask God to heal him.[7] If, without any preparation, she had to face the truth that he would die in nine months, she would have collapsed under the overwhelming weight of life without my father. God prepared her for my father's death during the nine months she spent time in prayers.

As we have seen, there are some benefits of self-deception primarily as a defense mechanism against pain. However, overall, the cost of

---

3. Ten Elshof, *I Told Me So*, 100.
4. Kirsch, "What's So Great," 422.
5. Kirsch, "What's So Great," 425.
6. Caldwell, "Identity, Self-Awareness," 396.
7. Every Korean church in South Korea offers dawn prayer meeting services Monday through Saturday about 5 a.m. or 5:30 a.m. Some big churches have more than one dawn prayer meeting services, typically at 5 a.m. and 6 a.m.

self-deception far outweighs any benefit we may gain from it. Self-deception about our moral character and conduct may facilitate vicious actions, sometimes with disastrous consequences, corrupt our conscience, and hinder our ability to change.

STRATEGIES OF SELF-DECEPTION

Strategies we employ for self-deception include attention management, procrastination, perspective switching, rationalization, and ressentiment.[8] We select what we pay attention to in order to maintain our false beliefs just as my mother refused to think about the likelihood of her husband's impending death. We procrastinate doing what our moral belief demands of us and gradually the belief disappears. For example, I know I need to support my suffering brothers and sisters in countries torn by war, persecution, famine, and natural disasters more consistently than just giving my tithe and donating to relief organizations occasionally. I think about how I need to come up with a better plan I can implement to give more sacrificially and consistently. But I procrastinate. Then tyranny of urgency takes over and my mind is occupied with day-to-day responsibilities of work, family, and other obligations. Procrastination joins forces with attention management. I manage my attention away from what I know will require more sacrifice on my part. Perspective switching is a means of diverting attention from an uncomfortable truth, and rationalization uses distorted reasoning to justify false beliefs and behaviors. During the nine months of my father's hospitalization, our family did not talk about preparing for his death. We focused our conversation on what we could do to help him recover. Ressentiment is a reordering of the sentiment by adjusting our affections, sentiments, and value judgments to avoid severe disappointment or self-censure.[9] Our family pretended that everything was going to be okay and did not show any sorrow or fear at the prospect of losing my father.

Other than my family's case of refusing to face the truth and instead engaging in group self-deception, there can be other understandable reasons for self-deception such as a desire to feel good about ourselves and our situations, stay motivated, make ourselves more presentable, get along with others, etc.

---

8. Ten Elshof, *I Told Me So*, 31–74.
9. Ten Elshof, *I Told Me So*, 31–74.

COLLECTIVE SELF-DECEPTION

As was the case of my family, there is collective self-deception.[10] Collective self-deception might refer simply to a group of similarly self-deceived individuals or to a group entity that is self-deceived. It raises a number of significant questions such as whether individuals within groups bear responsibility for their self-deception or for the part they play in the group's self-deception. Collective self-deception is a serious problem that demands our attention, given its capacity to entrench false beliefs and magnify their consequences, sometimes with tragic results. Left unchecked, it can do an incalculable amount of damage to groups including religious communities.

The Branch Davidians were a cult group that engaged in group self-deception in their belief that Mount Carmel in Waco, Texas, was the Davidic kingdom and David Koresh was the Christ. It ended in the tragic deaths of seventy-five members during a siege by the FBI in 1993.[11] Collective self-deception can take on a more subtle form than that of the Branch Davidians but is still just as tragic from the eternal perspective. Today, there are many sects and denominations that profess faith in Jesus Christ but reject his deity as taught in the Scriptures. Jehovah's Witnesses believe Jesus was a lesser god created by God the Father. Mormons believe that Jesus is one of many gods who used to be a human and his Father was also a human before he became a god. Unitarians deny the deity of Jesus. These are only a few examples of those who consider themselves Christians and profess faith in Jesus but do not believe him to be God the Son, the second person of the Trinity. When the true Jesus is rejected, then there is no salvation: "And there is salvation in no one else, for there is no other name under heaven given among men by which we must be saved" (Acts 4:12).

OVERCOMING SELF-DECEPTION

By God's Provision

Self-deception may be considered harmless enough when it simply involves a more positive view of our situations and our intelligence or competence, but often it involves rationalizing unethical behaviors and denying

---

10. DeWeese-Boyd, "Collective Self-Deception," 588–94.
11. Editors of Encyclopaedia Britannica, "Waco Siege."

complicity in criminal acts.[12] It was self-deceived, self-righteous religious leaders who often persecuted God's prophets and killed Jesus. Because self-deception stems from a sinful heart, dealing with self-deception must involve acknowledgment and confession of our sinfulness. Augustine believed that self-deception is a cognitive distortion resulting from sinful behavior, and moral virtue is necessary for intellectual excellence.[13] Sinful behavior will undermine our ability to judge whether we are unduly influenced by a deficient standard of goodness.[14] Floyd contends that the love of God can prevent self-deception—those who love God with singlemindedness have clear minds not clouded by misdirected passion and thus will be able to know the truth and have clear self-understanding.[15] The remedy for self-deception also does not so much lie in our own self-reflective capacities as in moral transformation made possible by the love of God.[16] God illuminates the minds of those who love him, and they then can see themselves clearly, being freed from self-deception. Floyd's thinking is consistent with the biblical teaching that the solution to the problem of sin does not lie in our willpower but in God's provision of freedom from the penalty and power of sin through the redemptive work of Christ and the work of the Holy Spirit.

Dealing with self-deception then must begin with acknowledging our propensity for self-deception and our inability to know our hearts, thus relying on God to reveal it to us: "Search me, O God, and know my heart! Try me and know my thoughts! And see if there be any grievous way in me, and lead me in the way everlasting!" (Ps 139:23–24). We need to seek the divine revelation in the Scriptures that enlightens the human mind and helps us see ourselves in a way that is consistent with reality. In this way, the darkness of self-deception is confronted by the enlightenment of God's revelation.[17] Only special revelation can unravel the depths of the human heart (Heb 4:12) and the idols present there.[18]

---

12. Floyd, "How to Cure Self-Deception," 66.
13. Floyd, "How to Cure Self-Deception," 62.
14. Floyd, "How to Cure Self-Deception," 65.
15. Floyd, "How to Cure Self-Deception," 77.
16. Floyd, "How to Cure Self-Deception," 77.
17. Geske, "Solidarity in the Fall," 95.
18. Geske, "Solidarity in the Fall," 95.

By Communal Life

As an important means of enlisting God's help, we should seek the help of others through communal life. Communal life in a believing community that practices spiritual disciplines of Scripture engagement, prayer, and confession is vitally important to keep self-deception at bay. This would involve joining a church that accurately teaches and practices the word of God since the word of God is what God prescribes to prevent self-deception (Deut 11:16–32). God's word is the Spirit's primary means to expose lies and shed light on the truth (Heb 4:12–13). Communal life also involves being a member of a healthy group of believers who love one another and are not afraid to confront one another's sins with courageous honesty. Confession is the first step toward acknowledging our sins (Jas 5:16), our lies to justify our sins, and our self-deception that covers up our lies. Prayer enlists divine assistance in the supernatural realm where Satan and his minions are actively working to blind human minds through deception (John 8:44; 2 Cor 4:3–4, "And even if our gospel is veiled, it is veiled to those who are perishing. In their case the god of this world has blinded the minds of the unbelievers, to keep them from seeing the light of the gospel of the glory of Christ, who is the image of God"; cf. 2 Thess 2:9–12).

By Persevering through Trials

We are naturally motivated to protect ourselves from pain. The Spirit can use this motivation to draw us to God as the true means of protection. Psalm 94:22 views God as the rock of our refuge, and 1 Pet 5:7 invites us to cast our anxieties on him. God uses suffering to draw us out of our self-centered concerns to a God-centered life. While self-deception keeps us from knowing the truth about ourselves and God, acceptance of our suffering can help us fight self-deception. How can suffering help us fight self-deception?

Trials are an integral part of the Christian life because they are the vehicle for the acquisition of self-knowledge.[19] Trials force us to choose between the love of God and self, and they reveal the true inclination of the heart and thus serve as the test of the genuineness of the professed faith. In this way, trials are the vehicle for the acquisition of self-knowledge.[20] Endurance in trials and persecutions provides opportunities to become aware

---

19. Chamberlain, "Self-Deception," 541–56.
20. Chamberlain, "Self-Deception," 553.

of and overcome self-deception through a commitment to trust God and his revealed truth rather than follow our reasoning and desires. Such trust in God's truth with the help of the Spirit can also enable us to reorder our desires and achieve a rationality that is oriented to truth and goodness.[21] Trials have purifying effects on our souls. To avoid self-deception, a commitment to seek and love the truth with courage and willingness to suffer is necessary.

Self-deception can have destructive results if one persists in it during trials of faith. History has shown what can happen when Christians try to maintain their faith without the willingness to pay the necessary price for their faith:

> Auschwitz stands as a symbol of one extreme to which our self-deception can lead. For the complicity of Christians with Auschwitz did not begin with their failure to object to the first slightly antisemitic laws and actions. It rather began when Christians assumed that they could be the heirs and carriers of the symbols of the faith without sacrifice and suffering.[22]

God often uses suffering in life to draw us out of our self-deception by revealing what is in our hearts, leading us to repentance and righteousness, which in turn allows us to know God and thereby ourselves better (cf. Heb 12:10–11, 14). Refusing to suffer for the truth can have disastrous consequences for our spirituality and to the world around us as demonstrated by the German church under the Nazi regime. Kierkegaard warns against failing to "invest your life upon that which lasts: to love God in truth, come what may, with the consequence that in this life you will suffer under the hands of men. Therefore, do not deceive yourself! Of all deceivers fear most yourself!"[23]

How do we ensure our salvation in the face of self-deception that has been ubiquitous in humanity since the fall? A scientific hypothesis is confirmed not by one isolated test, but by the aggregate results of repeated experimentation, and this accumulation of evidence eventually points to a recognizable pattern of behavior and a fixed habit. Perseverance in the Christian faith serves as the ground for self-assessment. Perseverance is the adequate foundation for a truly gracious assurance of salvation.[24] The

---

21. Sedgwick, "Redemption and Self-Deception," 409.
22. Burrell and Hauerwas, "Self-Deception and Autobiography," 100.
23. Kierkegaard, *Provocations*, 47.
24. Chamberlain, "Self-Deception," 553–55. Psychoanalysis may help uncover

author of Hebrews issues repeated warnings against apostasy because perseverance is the mark of genuine saving faith. Persecutions and other hardships in life provide opportunities to demonstrate genuineness of our faith (1 Cor 11:19; Jas 1:12; 1 Pet 1:7).

For Augustine, overcoming innate self-deception about his righteousness was a vital stage in his conversion from sinfulness to godliness because only when he came to accept that he was sinful did he see the need for a savior who could save him from his sins.[25] To be free from self-deception, we must love the truth because self-deception occurs when we know the truth and reject it or suppress it. Loving the truth leads to loving God since God is the ultimate truth, and when we love God, our loves become properly ordered. Loving God with undivided love will keep us from being clouded by sinful desires, and it will enable us to understand the truth about God and ourselves. But when we have idolatrous self-love, we will deny the truth of our sinfulness and creatureliness. The false cover story of self-sufficiency enables us to deny our need for God.

Ultimately, freedom from self-deception can come through Jesus Christ. Since it takes the work of the Holy Spirit to reveal to us true knowledge of ourselves by penetrating the deepest dimension of human hearts, we need to place ourselves in the community where the Spirit of God is working through the body of Christ. Most importantly, we need to abide in his word so that Christ can dwell in our hearts richly (Col 3:16), and his Spirit through his word can do the work of enlightening and transforming us as we behold his glory: "And we all, with unveiled face, beholding the glory of the Lord, are being transformed into the same image from one degree of glory to another. For this comes from the Lord who is the Spirit" (2 Cor 3:18). This gradual transformation accompanies gradual freedom from sin and self-deception.

---

self-deception. Christopher Kam suggests that Christian theology can be integrated with Jungian psychoanalysis, and he offers ways to utilize psychoanalysis in an integrative treatment (Kam, "Overcoming Self-Deception," 148–49).

25. Badgett, "Undermining Moral Self-Deception," 31.

6

Summary

IN THIS CHAPTER, I will summarize the book's content on self-deception in the Bible for a quick reference to each of the passages we discussed.

SELF-DECEPTION IN THE OLD TESTAMENT

What does the Bible say about self-deception? In both the Old and the New Testaments, self-deception is closely linked with the corruption and deceitfulness of the heart. We do not know the depth of our hearts, which is the Bible's way of saying that much goes on in our subconscious mind that our conscious mind is not fully aware of. God holds us accountable for the sinful thoughts and decisions made in our hearts because we are the ones who are choosing those thoughts and making those decisions even though we keep them from our consciousness.

Pentateuch

Genesis 3:1–13 shows that Satan's deception and Eve's self-deception worked together to induce her and Adam to eat the forbidden fruit. Satan used the partial truth that they would become like God if they ate the fruit, getting to know good and evil, and Eve reasoned that the fruit looked good for food and wisdom, and she desired it. This desire of her heart was deceitful because it arose out of her unbelief in God's word and belief in Satan's lie. Instead of bringing her the wisdom she hoped to acquire, it only brought moral autonomy and estrangement from God and reality. Desiring what God forbids stemming from the failure to trust God, along with the pride of self-importance, brought about the first sin in humanity. The self-deception of Adam and Eve turned the fatal temptation of Satan into an invitation for fulfillment and wisdom. Human history has been one of following the footsteps of our first ancestors in declaring moral autonomy from God and creating our own values and reality in our self-deceived belief that we can achieve fulfillment in life apart from God.

Deuteronomy 11:16 connects self-deception to idolatry. We worship idols when we allow our hearts to be deceived out of our sinful desires. We worship the gods we create in our image. The people of Israel rejected their identity as the people redeemed by God and found the Canaanite gods more appealing to them because these gods could be appeased and manipulated in a way that YHWH could not. Canaanite worship, known for its immorality, also appealed to their base desires. God holds self-deceivers accountable because self-deception is a failure of self-knowledge and rationality out of a willful choice to reject God and his truth. God prescribes his word as a preventative against self-deception (Deut 11:18–32).

Poetical Literature

Job 15:3 calls putting one's trust in anything other than God self-deception because God is the only one who can be trusted and relied upon without failure. Ironically, Eliphaz, who makes this statement, is himself self-deceived when he makes false accusations against Job. Eliphaz was not trusting God but his faulty reasoning. In Job 31:33, Job shows his awareness of the dangers of being self-deceived and turning a blind eye to his sins. Job lists self-deception along with other serious sins such as injustice, idolatry, and enemy hate (vv. 5–29).

According to Prov 12:15, self-deception is a failure of accurate self-assessment, and this is connected to the failure to receive honest feedback from others. A self-deceived person does not listen to wise counsel. Good and transparent relationships with wise and caring people can mitigate self-deception as they speak the truth into our lives and help us see ourselves without distortion. Proverbs repeatedly warns against being wise in our own eyes because it constitutes a failure of self-knowledge (26:5, 12, 16; 28:11).

Summary

Proverbs 14:8 equates wisdom with self-awareness and folly with self-deception. In self-deception, the way to death can appear as the right way (Prov 16:25). Such cognitive failure is caused by the moral failure of not shunning evil. In Proverbs, the fear of the Lord is the beginning of knowledge and the means to attaining a fulfilling life, and it is consistently connected to shunning evil (8:13; 16:6; 23:17). Self-deception, on the other hand, is connected to the moral failure of not shunning evil. We believe what we want to believe against the evidence because our sinful desires take delight in unrighteousness.

Prophetic Literature

Isaiah 5:20–21 shows that distorted self-understanding leads people to a distorted understanding of God—there is a close connection between self-knowledge and the knowledge of God. To be wise in our own eyes, we have to reject God's truth and create our own version of wisdom and folly, right and wrong, and good and evil. Those who reject God's word live in self-deception and create their own version of God. Those who delight in unrighteousness still want to consider themselves righteous, so they change what righteousness looks like, redefining reality to prevent being confronted by it. In the process, they remake God in their image.

Isaiah 44:20 depicts the folly of idolatry as a man carving a piece of wood into an idol and falling down to worship it. He has chosen to shut his eyes and refuse to understand with his heart. Self-deception is voluntary and intentional, but he cannot deliver himself from this folly because his heart has been deceived. Since this idolatry out of self-deception is rejection of the true God and rebellion against him, God judges it by allowing him to have a dull heart that does not understand the truth nor turn to God to be healed (Isa 6:9–10). Self-deception then is our fault resulting from our sin but at the same time God's judgment on those who reject God and his truth (65:2–5). Nothing escapes God's sovereignty including our self-deception.

In Jer 2:34–35, sinners deny their wrongdoing, protest their innocence, and convince themselves that God is not angry with them. Self-deception involves holding a belief against the evidence by using faulty reasoning. Deeply held beliefs in subconsciousness about their sinfulness are repressed or carefully avoided from the attention of the conscious mind to maintain a façade of rationality in maintaining their innocence.

Jeremiah 17:9 addresses the condition of the heart that is corrupt and deceitful. It is unsearchable even to its owner. This failure to know our hearts is motivated by our unwillingness to face the truth about our sinfulness and our desire to view ourselves as good without having to acknowledge our moral failures and guilty standing before God. Selfishness is at the core of our failure to know our hearts because our selfish desire to view ourselves as good distorts our moral reasoning, which leads to our cognitive failure to know ourselves accurately. Our selfishness trains us to become very good at self-justification and at the same time allows us to continue to pursue sinful desires. Rather than discerning the truth, we much prefer to create our own reality in which our excellences are magnified and our defects are diminished. In this virtual reality, everything appears in false colors. Falsehood becomes truth and righteousness becomes wickedness (cf. Prov 29:27). We do everything in our power to conceal the truth about ourselves from surfacing to our consciousness. No wonder our heart is inaccessible to us apart from divine aid.

Jeremiah 37:9 shows self-deception at play in the people of Judah as they tell themselves that the Babylonians will go away from them and no longer pose a threat to the nation. Thoughtfully weighing the evidence would not allow them to come to such a conclusion, but it was too painful for them to face the truth of God's coming judgment and their exile to Babylon. To suppress the truth, they make Jeremiah a false prophet and a traitor. Though they knew Jeremiah to be a prophet sent by God, their pride did not allow them to concede to Jeremiah's prophecies about the coming judgment by God, so they tried to kill Jeremiah. There were many things that they could use to bolster their self-deception such as their status as the covenant people of God and God's unconditional promises to Abraham and his descendants. Their idolatry and oppression of the poor among other sins that would soon cause God's judgment and their downfall were conveniently ignored. Micah had prophesied more than a hundred years before Jeremiah's time about the coming judgment (Mic 3:11–12), but the slow nature of God's judgment was used by the people of Judah to strengthen their self-deception rather than as an opportunity for repentance.

In summary, the Old Testament points out the close connection between self-deception and the fallenness of the human heart manifesting in selfish desires and pride, and rejection of God's righteousness and truth all the while maintaining the façade of godliness and righteousness. Moral failure causes cognitive failure of self-knowledge.

Summary

SELF-DECEPTION IN THE NEW TESTAMENT

The New Testament often addresses the self-deception of those who profess faith without having genuine faith. Jesus taught that the believing community would be a mixed community of genuine and false believers (Matt 22:1–14; 25:1–13). Scholars describe the latter in various ways such as "false followers," "professing Christians," or "superficial disciples." Paul addresses false believers often in his letters, asking the readers to examine their faith (2 Cor 13:5) and warning them that it is possible to be deceived about inheriting the kingdom of God (1 Cor 6:9–10; Gal 5:19–21; Eph 5:5–6). General Epistles also warn against alleged faith that shows no evidence of its genuineness (Jas 2:14–26). The false believers that the New Testament addresses are self-deceived about their faith and their eternal destiny.

Gospels and Acts

In Matt 7:21–23, Jesus warns that many who call him Lord will not enter the kingdom of God because they never had personal relationships with him and their deeds are sinful, but they are self-deceived about their prospect of entering the kingdom because of their ministry credentials. False believers look very much like genuine believers on the surface, which increases the danger of their self-deception.

Luke 8:11–15 contains Jesus' interpretation of the parable of the sower. Among the four soils in the parable, the first one, the path, represents those who hear the word but do not believe, and the fourth one, the good soil, represents those who hear the word and understand it, bearing the fruit of salvation. The second and third soils, the rocky soil and thorny bushes, represent the hearers of the word who believe in superficial ways without the right heart and true understanding, so they fall away during times of trials or let the cares and pleasures of life choke the word out of their hearts. It would be self-deception if these hearers only think that they are saved when their hearts are not right and there is no fruit of salvation.

In Luke 18:9–14, Jesus tells a parable about a self-righteous Pharisee and a repentant tax collector praying at the temple to teach that it is the tax collector who is justified by God, not the Pharisee, because God saves sinners but self-righteousness is self-deception that refuses to acknowledge one's sinfulness. Luke's theme of the reversal of fortune is closely related to the biblical theme of self-deception. Jesus pronounces scathing rebukes on hypocrites who are self-deceived about their righteousness. This Pharisee in the parable is an example of a hypocrite.

John 8:33 shows the self-deception of those who claim to be descendants of Abraham and free from any enslavement in response to Jesus' words that if they abide in his word, then they will know the truth and the truth will set them free. Though John says that they believed in Jesus in 8:30–31, the ensuing dialogue between them and Jesus shows that their faith is only superficial because they do not really believe him (8:45), their father is the devil (v. 44), and they are not of God (v. 47). Though it is easy enough for someone to be attracted to Jesus in a superficial way and think that he or she believes in Jesus, Jesus says that abiding in his word is the test of genuine faith. Perseverance is what separates self-deceived false believers from genuine believers.

In Acts 8:9–24, Luke tells the account of Simon the magician's supposed conversion and subsequent curse by Peter. Though he "believed" and was baptized, his interaction with Peter shows that Simon was a false believer. When Simon sees people receiving the Holy Spirit, he offers money to Peter to buy the power to confer the Spirit, seeing an opportunity for material gain through this power (vv. 18–19). Peter sees that Simon's heart is not right before God and is not sure whether Simon can be forgiven because he is enslaved to sin (vv. 21–23). Simon would be a case of a self-deceived false believer if he was sincere in his belief and baptism, as Luke seems to portray him, even though his was a superficial faith.

Pauline Epistles

Before Paul met Jesus on the road to Damascus, he was self-deceived in his belief that he was blameless in his righteous standing before the law and that he was serving God by persecuting Christians. Naturally, Paul shows concerns about those in the church who are self-deceived about their faith. In Rom 1:18–23, Paul addresses the self-deception of unbelievers who claim to know God but suppress the truth about God and turn to idol worship in their unrighteousness. Self-deception is first volitional before it is cognitive. Sinners do not know the truth because they suppress it. So they are culpable for their self-deception. Exchanging the truth of God for a lie has been the pattern of sinful humanity since Adam and Eve, and self-deception plays a key role in this exchange—claiming to be wise, they became fools. As in the Old Testament, self-deception is a result of divine judgment—God hands sinners over to their choice to reject God and to its consequences (Rom 1:24, 26, 28; 11:8, 10).

In Rom 2:13, Paul says that those who are hearers of the law without being doers of the law are self-deceived in their belief that they know God and the truth. Their claim to be the teachers of the law only shows their hypocrisy since they break the law and dishonor God (v. 23). If they think their circumcision gives them a secure status as Jews (the covenant people of God), they are self-deceived since a true Jew is the one who is circumcised in the heart by the Spirit (v. 29). Relying on external status leads to self-deception since what truly matters is the inner state of the heart.

In Rom 7:13—8:17, Paul recounts his utter failure in the struggle against sin as he attempted to obey the law without the Spirit's enablement. As a Jew, he had a cover story of his blamelessness concerning the law (Phil 3:6) and a real story of helplessness in sin's enslavement (Rom 7:14). Paul uses the present tense verbs in Rom 7:14–25 to depict Israel's ongoing experience of life under the law, but he also may be addressing the struggles of the false believers in the church. Paul says that he delights in the law of God in his inner being in 7:22 but that the mind set on the flesh is hostile to God in 8:7. This is the way a self-deceived mind operates—with a cover story and a true story underneath it. As a zealous Jew, he delighted in the law of God, but the truth was that his mind was hostile to God, so he rejected Jesus and persecuted his followers. Paul distinguishes between those who are in the flesh without the Spirit and those who are putting to death the deeds of the body with the help of the Holy Spirit. This contrast between the unregenerate and the regenerate is also the contrast between the false believers and genuine believers in the church. Paul warns that anyone who does not have the Spirit of Christ does not belong to him (8:9b).

In 1 Cor 3:18, Paul admonishes the Corinthians not to deceive themselves into thinking they are wise when in fact they are exhibiting spiritual immaturity. Such self-exaltation in self-deception was causing divisions in the church. In 1 Cor 4:5, Paul asks the Corinthians not to judge him too hastily since when the Lord returns, he will judge the hidden purposes of the heart. Paul does not judge himself as he is not aware of anything against himself, but that does not mean that he is exonerated since he could be self-deceived about his innocence. Only the Lord knows what is hidden in his heart and will reveal it on the day of judgment. This means too much introspection and self-doubt is not helpful. After careful self-reflection, we

What the Bible Says about the Dangers of Self-Deception

need to let God be the judge of our deepest motives as they are not accessible to us for now.

Paul issues a strong warning in 1 Cor 6:9 to those who are self-deceived that they will inherit the kingdom of God while living lives that are characterized by sin. The gravity of the consequence of self-deception is pronounced here since eternal destiny is at stake. Naturally, Paul is concerned about those in his churches who may not enter the kingdom of God. We should also be mindful and concerned about the existence of false believers in our churches and be strategic about bringing them into the kingdom.

In 2 Cor 13:5–7 Paul tells the Corinthian believers to examine and test themselves to see if they are in the faith. If Christ is not in them, they are not genuine believers (cf. Rom 8:9). The word Paul uses to describe those who are not genuine believers is ἀδόκιμοί (*adokimoi*) and it means a "counterfeit" or "tested and proven false." The opposite word is δόκιμοι (*dokimoi*), which means "tested and proven genuine." These words appear many times in Pauline Epistles and the rest of the New Testament letters to describe those who are tested and proven to be either false or genuine believers. It shows that New Testament authors are thinking about their churches as mixed communities of genuine and false believers. Since false believers are self-deceived into believing that they are genuine believers, many warnings are issued against being deceived (e.g., Gal 6:3, 7; 1 Cor 6:9–10; Jas 1:16, 22; 1 John 1:8). The New Testament's emphasis on the need for the fruit, manifestations of the Spirit versus flesh, and warnings against apostasy can be seen in this connection also.

Galatians 6:1–10 shows Paul's concern about those who are in the church but still in the flesh and thus will not inherit eternal life (v. 8; cf. 5:19–21). Paul warns against self-deception twice in this passage (6:3, 7–8). In verse 3, self-deception is about one's unfounded self-exaltation, and in verses 7–8, it is about inheriting eternal life while sowing to the flesh, that is, habitual sin characterizing their lives. The danger of self-deception is that those who are engaged in the works of the flesh can deceive themselves into believing that they are doing important and spiritual works (6:3), not realizing that they may not even inherit eternal life.

In 2 Thess 2:9–12, Paul writes powerfully about the culpability of those who are self-deceived because they refuse to love the truth and delight in unrighteousness. Rational failure and moral failure are closely connected. Out of their sinful desires, sinners rationalize immoral behaviors. Self-deception is also the result of divine judgment (v. 11) and the outworking of divine justice in response to people's rejection of the truth and God and their choice of falsehood and sin. Sinners' defiance of God and his truth becomes the means of God's judgment as he delivers them to the deception of Satan (vv. 9–11).

Hebrews and General Epistles

The author of Hebrews has two groups of people in mind—genuine and false believers—and he provides assurance of salvation to the former (6:9–10; 10:39), not based on their ability to maintain their faith but on Christ's finished work of atonement and ongoing work of intercession for them as the perfecter of their salvation (12:2) and as their faithful high priest (9:26–28). They have already entered God's rest (4:9–10) and come to the heavenly Jerusalem (12:22). To the false believers, the author warns about the danger of eternal judgment (6:4–8; 10:26–31) because of their unbelief and hardening of their hearts (3:8, 15; 4:7). They have not entered God's rest (4:1, 11) and have not obtained God's grace (12:15). Because they hardened their hearts, the new covenant promises of a new heart and forgiveness of sins have not become a reality for them.

Hebrews 3:13 warns against being hardened by the deceitfulness of sin. Sinful desires are deceitful in that they cover up their sinfulness and justify them as acceptable desires. In the Bible, hardening is almost always about the hardening of the heart against God, so the warning is against apostasy. In Heb 4:1–11, the author warns the individuals among the readers who have failed to enter God's rest, which is a metaphor for salvation experience, because of the hardening of their heart in unbelief. The author sees a close parallel between the wilderness generation who failed to enter the promised land because of their unbelief and the self-deceived false believers among his readers. They are also in danger of failing to enter God's rest due to their hardening of hearts in unbelief when they hear God's voice (3:15; 4:7). They have not experienced the new covenant blessing of a new heart. For the author of Hebrews, just as Moses and Jeremiah before him, the heart is the central issue that determines one's covenant relationship with God. Those who harden their hearts and do not subject themselves to God's discipline are illegitimate children—they do not belong to God (Heb 12:8). They are self-deceived false believers.

James 1:22 warns against the self-deception of being hearers of the word only and not doers, which leads to false self-reckoning such as being wise in one's own eyes (Prov 26:12). The central theme of the letter of James is the need for genuine faith that manifests itself in life (Jas 2:14–26). Without such manifestation, any claim to have faith and salvation is self-deceived. James 1:26 states that those who think they are religious but do not bridle their tongues are deceiving their hearts. Controlling one's speech is a sign of the Spirit's work of regeneration. For Jesus, one's speech shows the state of the heart whether good or evil (Luke 6:45). Uncontrolled speech of those who claim to be spiritual shows they are deceiving themselves. They are controlled by their sinful desires rather than by God's word.

In 2:14–26, James delineates what genuine saving faith looks like and warns those who think they can be saved with an alleged faith that is no different from the faith of demons. It would be a dangerous self-deception to believe that a deficient faith that does not accompany works (the outworkings or fruit of saving faith) can save its possessor. James provides examples of Abraham and Rahab to demonstrate that any claim to faith that is not lived out in life is useless since such faith does not justify its possessors and cannot save them.

In 1 John 1:8, John says that if we claim to be sinless, we are deceiving ourselves. In his letter, John is addressing the secessionists who left his church and started their own with their own Christology that denied Christ's humanity and the incarnation. This led to their claim to be sinless while practicing sin (1:8, 10; 3:4–10), because they rejected the significance of their immoral deeds in their belief that only the spirit lives on and their bodies would be done away with. They were influenced by Greek dualism that considered matter (including the body) as evil or irrelevant. These secessionists show the danger of self-deception that promoted a false gospel that was leading themselves and their converts to eternal destruction.

Two of the reasons why the self-deceived are held accountable are that self-deception is a failure of self-knowledge and a failure of rationality. It is morally wrong to believe something out of selfish desires or pride based on insufficient evidence and without investigation. Self-deception about our immorality leads us to commit more immoral actions by rationalizing morally questionable and reprehensible choices and actions. This explains much of our sinful behaviors and our refusal to acknowledge our sins. Self-knowledge is the beginning of all human wisdom, and much biblical discussion of self-deception is concerned with the lack of self-knowledge.

The Scripture teaches that self-deception is a failure to know ourselves accurately (the opposite of self-knowledge), is closely related to sin, stems

Summary

from disordered love for self (pride and selfish desires), and prevents people from knowing and loving God because self-deception suppresses the truth, and we cannot find God apart from the truth. Communal life in a believing community that practices spiritual disciplines of Scripture engagement, prayer, and confession and endurance through trials and persecutions provide opportunities to become aware of and overcome self-deception. Ultimately, it is the Holy Spirit who uses the word of God, communal life, and trials to enlighten and transform us to free us from self-deception.

Bibliography

Alden, Robert L. *Job*. The New American Commentary 11. Nashville: Broadman & Holman, 1993.
———. *Proverbs*. Grand Rapids: Baker Book House, 1983.
Allen, David M. "'The Forgotten Spirit': A Pentecostal Reading of the Letter to the Hebrews?" *Journal of Pentecostal Theology* 18 (2009) 51–66.
Alton, Bruce. "The Morality of Self-Deception." *Annual of the Society of Christian Ethics* 5 (1985) 123–55.
Andersen, Francis I. *Job*. Tyndale Old Testament Commentaries 14. Downers Grove, IL: InterVarsity, 2008.
Attridge, Harold W. *Hebrews*. Hermeneia. Philadelphia: Fortress, 1989.
Augustine. *Confessions*. Translated by J. G. Pilkington. https://www.logoslibrary.org/augustine/confessions/1032.html.
Badgett, Jonathan Paul. "Christian Self-Knowledge: A Christological Framework for Undermining Dissociation through Reconciliation." PhD diss., Southern Baptist Theological Seminary, 2018.
———. "Undermining Moral Self-Deception with the Help of Puritan Pastoral Theology." *Journal of Spiritual Formation and Soul Care* 11.1 (2018) 23–38. https://doi.org/10.1177/1939790917749305.
Bahnsen, Greg. "The Crucial Concept of Self-Deception in Presuppositional Apologetics." *Westminster Theological Journal* 57 (1995) 1–31.
Baron, Marcia. "What Is Wrong with Self-Deception." In *Perspectives on Self-Deception*, edited by Brian P. McLaughlin and Amelie O. Rorty, 431–49. Berkeley: University of California Press, 1988.
Barrett, C. K. *A Critical and Exegetical Commentary on the Acts of the Apostles*. International Critical Commentary. Edinburgh: T&T Clark, 1994.
Barth, Karl. *Church Dogmatics*. Edited by G. W. Bromily and T. F. Torrance. Translated by J. W. Edwards et al. Vol. 4. Edinburgh: T&T Clark, 1958.
Bateman, Herbert, IV, ed. *Four Views of the Warning Passages in Hebrews*. Grand Rapids: Kregel, 2007.
Bauer, Walter, et al. *Greek-English Lexicon of the New Testament and Other Early Christian Literature*. 3rd ed. Chicago: University of Chicago Press, 2000.

Bibliography

Beasley-Murray, George R. *John*. Word Biblical Commentary 36. Waco, TX: Word Books, 1987.

Billon, Alexandre. "Have We Vindicated the Motivational Unconscious Yet? A Conceptual View." *Frontiers in Psychology: Psychoanalysis and Neuropschoanalysis* 2 (Sept. 2011) 1–20.

Bird, Michael F. *Romans*. The Story of God Bible Commentary. Grand Rapids: Zondervan, 2016.

Blomberg, Craig L. *Neither Poverty nor Riches: A Biblical Theology of Material Possessions*. Edited by D. A. Carson. New Studies in Biblical Theology. Grand Rapids: Eerdmans, 1999.

Bock, Darrell L. *Luke: 9:51—24:53*. Vol. 2. Baker Exegetical Commentary on the New Testament. Grand Rapids: Baker Books, 1996.

Botha, Pieter J. J. "Theology, Rationality and Truth-Claims: Metatheoretical Reflections on Self-Deception." *Religion and Theology* 12.2 (2005) 97–128.

Brosend, William F. *James and Jude*. New Cambridge Bible Commentary. Cambridge: Cambridge University Press, 2004.

Brown, Francis, et al. *Hebrew and English Lexicon of the Old Testament*. Oxford: Clarendon, 1907.

Bruce, F. F. *The Epistle to the Galatians*. The New International Greek Testament Commentary. Grand Rapids: Eerdmans, 1982.

———. *The Epistle to the Hebrews*. The International Commentary on the New Testament. Grand Rapids: Eerdmans, 1964.

Burrell, David, and Stanley Hauerwas. "Self-Deception and Autobiography: Theological and Ethical Reflections on Speer's Inside the Third Reich." *Journal of Religious Ethics* 2 (Spring 1974) 99–117.

Butler, Joseph. "Sermon X. Upon Self-Deceit—2 Sam. xii. 7." Christian Classics Ethereal Library. https://ccel.org/ccel/butler/sermons/sermons.iii.x.html.

Caldwell, Cam. "Identity, Self-Awareness, and Self-Deception: Ethical Implications for Leaders and Organizations." *Journal of Business Ethics* 90 (2009) 393–406.

Calvin, John. *The Acts of the Apostles 1–13*. Translated by John W. Fraser and W. J. G. McDonald. Calvin's Commentaries. Grand Rapids: Eerdmans, 1965.

———. *Institutes of the Christian Religion*. Christian Classics Ethereal Library. https://www.ccel.org/ccel/calvin/institutes.toc.html.

Carson, D. A. *The Gospels according to John*. Grand Rapids: Eerdmans, 1991.

———. *Matthew: Chapters 1 through 12*. The Expositor's Bible Commentary. Grand Rapids: Zondervan, 1995.

Cerovac, Ivan. "Intentionalism as a Theory of Self-Deception." *Balkan Journal of Philosophy* 7.2 (Jan. 1, 2015) 145–50.

Chamberlain, Ava. "Self-Deception as a Theological Problem in Jonathan Edwards's 'Treatise Concerning Religious Affections.'" *Church History* 63.4 (Dec. 1994) 541–56.

Clifford, William K. "The Ethics of Belief." In *Lectures and Essays*, edited by Leslie Stephen and Frederick Pollock, 1–10. London: Macmillan, 1886. https://people.brandeis.edu/~teuber/Clifford_ethics.pdf.

Clines, David J. A. *Job 21–37*. Word Biblical Commentary 18A. Nashville: Thomas Nelson, 2006.

Cockerill, Gareth Lee. *The Epistle to the Hebrews*. The New International Commentary on the New Testament. Grand Rapids: Eerdmans, 2012.

Coe, John. "Intentional Spiritual Formation in the Classroom: Making Space for the Spirit in the University." *Christian Education Journal* 4NS (2000) 85–110.

Craigie, Peter C., Jr., et al. *Jeremiah 1–25*. Word Biblical Commentary 26. Dallas: Word Books, 1991.

Cranfield, C. E. B. "The Message of James." *Scottish Journal of Theology* 18 (Sept. 1965) 182–93, 338–45.

———. *Romans 1–8*. Vol. 1. The International Critical Commentary. Edinburgh: T&T Clark, 1975.

Davids, Peter. *Commentary on James*. New International Greek Testament Commentary. Grand Rapids: Eerdmans, 1982.

Demos, Raphael. "Lying to Oneself." *Journal of Philosophy* 57 (Sept. 1, 1960) 588–94.

DeWeese-Boyd, Ian. "Collective Self-Deception, Collective Injustice: Consumption, Sustainability and Responsibility." Paper presented at The Rocky Mountain Ethics Congress Center for Values and Social Policy, University of Colorado, 2008.

Dillow, Joseph C. *The Reign of the Servant Kings: A Study of Eternal Security and the Final Destiny of Man*. Miami Springs, FL: Schoettle, 1992.

Dings, Roy. "Social Strategies in Self-Deception." *New Ideas in Psychology* 47 (2017) 16–23.

Dunn, James D. G. *The Acts of the Apostles*. Epworth Commentaries. London: Epworth, 1996.

———. *Romans 1–8*. Word Biblical Commentary 38A. Dallas: Word Books, 1988.

Editors of Encyclopaedia Britannica. "Waco Siege." *Encyclopaedia Britannica*. Last updated September 16, 2024. https://www.britannica.com/event/Waco-siege.

Edwards, James R. *Romans*. New International Biblical Commentary. Peabody, MA: Hendrickson, 1992.

Edwards, Jonathan. *The Religious Affections*. Carlisle, PA: The Banner of Truth Trust, 1746.

Exell, Joseph S., ed. "The Impurity of the Heart." *The Biblical Illustrator*. https://biblehub.com/sermons/pub/the_impurity_of_the_heart.htm.

Fanning, Buist. "A Classical Reformed View." In *Four Views of the Warning Passages in Hebrews*, edited by Herbert Bateman IV, 172–219. Grand Rapids: Kregel, 2007.

Fee, Gordon D. *The First Epistle to the Corinthians*. The New International Commentary on the New Testament. Grand Rapids: Eerdmans, 1987.

———. *Paul, the Spirit, and the People of God*. Ada, MI: Baker Academic, 1996.

Fernández, Jordi. "Self-Deception and Self-Knowledge." *Philosophical Studies: An International Journal for Philosophy in the Analytic Tradition* 162.2 (Jan. 1, 2013) 379–400.

Fingarette, Herbert. *Self-Deception*. London: Routledge & Kegan Paul, 1969.

Fitzmyer, Joseph. *Romans*. The Anchor Bible 33. New York: Doubleday, 1993.

Floyd, Shawn D. "How to Cure Self-Deception: An Augustinian Remedy." *Logos: A Journal of Catholic Thought and Culture* 7.3 (2004) 60–86.

Fox, Michael V. *Proverbs 10–31*. The Anchor Yale Bible 18b. New Haven: Yale University Press, 2009.

France, R. T. *Matthew*. Tyndale New Testament Commentaries. Grand Rapids: Eerdmans, 1985.

Freud, Sigmund. *The Unconscious*. London: Penguin Classic, 2005.

Funkhouser, Eric. *Self-Deception*. New York: Routledge, 2019.

Geske, Andre. "Solidarity in the Fall: An Essay on Self-Deception." *Unio Cum Christo: International Journal of Reformed Theology and Life* 6.1 (Apr. 2020) 83–97.

Goldbert, Sanford C. "The Psychology and Epistemology of Self-Knowledge." *Synthese* 118 (1999) 165–99.
Green, Michael. *The Message of Matthew*. The Bible Speaks Today. Downers Grove, IL: IVP Academic, 2000.
Greene, Oliver B. *The Gospel according to Matthew*. Vol. 6. Greenville, SC: The Gospel Hour, 1975.
Gundry, Robert H. *Matthew: A Commentary on His Handbook for a Mixed Church under Persecution*. 2nd ed. Grand Rapids: Eerdmans, 1982.
Guthrie, George H. *2 Corinthians*. Baker Exegetical Commentary on the New Testament. Grand Rapids: Baker Academic, 2015.
———. *Hebrews*. The NIV Application Commentary. Grand Rapids: Zondervan, 1998.
Hållén, Elinor. "A Different Kind of Ignorance: Self-Deception as Flight from Self-Knowledge." PhD diss., Uppsala University, 2011.
Hartley, John E. *Genesis*. New International Biblical Commentary. Peabody, MA: Hendrickson, 2000.
Hiebert, D. Edmond. *1 and 2 Thessalonians*. Chicago: Moody Press, 1992.
———. "Unifying Theme of the Epistle of James." *Bibliotheca Sacra* 135.539 (July 1978) 221–31.
Hodges, Zane C. *Dead Faith: What Is It?* Dallas: Redencion, 1987.
House, Paul R. *Isaiah: A Mentor Commentary*. Vol. 1. Fern, Scot.: Mentor, 2019.
Johnson, Eric, and Christina Burroughs. "Protecting One's Soul: A Christian Inquiry into Defensive Activity." *Journal of Psychology and Theology* 28.3 (2000) 175–89.
Jung, Carl G. *Structure and Dynamics of the Psyche*. Collected Works of C. G. Jung 8. Princeton: Princeton University Press, 1970.
Kam, Christopher. "Overcoming Self-Deception: Integrating Christian Theology with Jungian Psychoanalysis." *Journal of Psychology and Christianity* 37.2 (Summer 2018) 137–52.
Keener, Craig S. *Galatians: A Commentary*. Grand Rapids: B&H Academic, 2019.
———. *Romans*. New Covenant Commentary Series. Eugene, OR: Cascade, 2009.
Kierkegaard, Søren. *Provocations: Spiritual Writings of Kierkegaard*. Edited by Charles E. Moore. Farmington, PA: Bruderhof Foundation, 2002. https://www.ldolphin.org/Provocations.pdf.
Kim, Seyoon, and F. F. Bruce. *1 and 2 Thessalonians*. 2nd ed. Word Biblical Commentary 45. Grand Rapids: Zondervan, 2023.
Kinghorn, Kevin Paul. "Spiritual Blindness, Self-Deception and Morally Culpable Nonbelief." *Heythrop Journal* 48.4 (July 2007) 527–45.
Kirsch, Julie. "What's So Great about Reality?" *Canadian Journal of Philosophy* 35.3 (Sept. 2005) 407–28.
Kruse, Colin G. *Paul's Letter to the Romans*. The Pillar New Testament Commentary. Grand Rapids: Eerdmans, 2012.
Lambert, Laura. "Stockholm Syndrome." *Encyclopaedia Britannica*. Last updated September 10, 2024. https://www.britannica.com/science/Stockholm-syndrome.
Lane, William. *Hebrews: A Call to Commitment*. Peabody, MA: Hendrickson, 1985.
Lauria, Federico, and Delphine Presismann. "What Does Emotion Teach Us about Self-Deception? Affective Neuroscience in Support of Non-Intentionalism." *The Ethics Forum* 13.2 (Summer 2018) 70–94.
Lehne, S. *The New Covenant in Hebrews*. Sheffield, UK: JSOT Press, 1990.

BIBLIOGRAPHY

Lenski, R. C. H. *The Interpretation of the Acts of the Apostles.* Columbus, OH: Wartburg, 1944.

Letham, Robert W. A. "Saving Faith and Assurance in Reformed Theology: Zwingli to the Synod of Dort." PhD diss., University of Aberdeen, 1979.

Levy, Neil. "Who's Fooling Who? Self-Deception and Addiction." *Res Publica* 11.1 (2002) 6–10.

Liubinskas, Susann M. *The Ethnographic Character of Romans: The Dichotomies of Law-Faith and Jew-Gentile in Light of Greco-Roman and Hellenistic Jewish Ethnography.* Eugene, OR: Pickwick, 2019.

Lockie, Robert. "Depth Psychology and Self-Deception." *Philosophical Psychology* 16.1 (2003) 127–48.

Mackay, John L. *Jeremiah: An Introduction and Commentary.* Vol. 1. Fearn, Scot.: Mentor, 2004.

Marshall, I. Howard. *Acts: An Introduction and Commentary.* Tyndale New Testament Commentaries. Downers Grove, IL: InterVarsity, 1980.

Matthews, Kenneth A. *Genesis 1—11:26.* The New American Commentary 1A. Nashville: Broadman & Holman, 1996.

McCartney, Dan. *James.* Baker Exegetical Commentary on the New Testament. Grand Rapids: Baker Academic, 2009.

Mele, Alfred. *Self-Deception Unmasked.* Princeton: Princeton University, 2001.

Merrill, Eugene H. *Deuteronomy.* The New American Commentary 4. Nashville: Broadman & Holman, 1994.

Moo, Douglas. *The Epistle to the Romans.* The New International Commentary on the New Testament. Grand Rapids: Eerdmans, 1996.

———. *Galatians.* Baker Exegetical Commentary on the New Testament. Grand Rapids: Baker Academic, 2013.

———. *James.* Rev. ed. Tyndale New Testament Commentaries. Grand Rapids: Eerdmans, 1987.

———. *The Letter of James.* The Pillar New Testament Commentary. Grand Rapids: Eerdmans, 2000.

Morris, Leon. *1 and 2 Thessalonians.* Rev. ed. Tyndale New Testament Commentaries. Grand Rapids: Eerdmans, 1984.

———. *The First and Second Epistles to the Thessalonians.* Rev. ed. The New International Commentary on the New Testament. Grand Rapids: Eerdmans, 1991.

———. *The Gospel according to John.* The New International Commentary on the New Testament. Grand Rapids: Eerdmans, 1971.

Motyer, Alec. *Isaiah: An Introduction and Commentary.* Downers Grove, IL: InterVarsity, 1999.

Mounce, Robert H. *Romans.* The New American Commentary 27. Nashville: Broadman & Holman, 1995.

Murphy, Roland E. *Proverbs.* Word Biblical Commentary 22. Nashville: Thomas Nelson, 1998.

Nicholson, Anna. "Cognitive Bias, Intentionality, and Self-Deception." *Teorema* 26.3 (2007) 45–58.

Oswald, Hilton C., ed. *Lectures on Romans.* Translated by Walter G. Tillmanns and Jacob A. O. Preus. Luther's Works 25. Saint Louis: Concordia, 1972.

Oswalt, John N. *The Book of Isaiah Chapters 1–39.* The New International Commentary on the Old Testament. Grand Rapids: Eerdmans, 1986.

Bibliography

Painter, John. *James*. Paideia Commentaries on the New Testament. Grand Rapids: Baker Academic, 2012.

Pak, Joseph K. "Assurance of Salvation in Hebrews." *American Journal of Biblical Theology* 24.31 (2023) 1–26. https://www.biblicaltheology.com/Research/PakJK03.pdf.

———. "Self-Deception in Current Philosophical Discussions and Its Importance in Theology." *International Journal of Philosophy and Theology* 4.1 (2016) 13–21.

———. "Self-Deception in Theology." *Themelios* 43.3 (Dec. 2018) 405–16.

———. "A Study of Selected Passages on Distinguishing Marks of Genuine and False Believers." PhD diss., Dallas Theological Seminary, 2001.

Pascal, Blaise. *Pensées*. Translated by A. J. Krailsheimer. New York: Penguin, 1966.

Plantinga, Cornelius, Jr. *Not the Way It's Supposed to Be: A Breviary of Sin*. Grand Rapids: Eerdmans, 1995.

Prenter, Regin. *Spiritus Creator*. Translated by John M. Jensen. Philadelphia: Muhlenberg, 1953.

Ridderbos, Herman N. *Matthew*. Translated by Ray Togtman. Bible Student's Commentary. Grand Rapids: Zondervan, 1987.

Ridderbos, J. *Isaiah*. Bible Student's Commentary. Grand Rapids: Zondervan, 1985.

Rodriguez, Jose David, Sr. "The Church: Sign and First Fruit of the Kingdom." *Currents in Theology and Mission* (Aug. 2002) 273–81.

Sailhamer, John H. *Genesis*. Rev. ed. The Expositor's Bible Commentary 1. Grand Rapids: Zondervan, 2008.

Schreiner, Thomas R. *Romans*. 2nd ed. Baker Exegetical Commentary on the New Testament. Grand Rapids: Baker Academic, 2018.

Sedgwick, Peter. "Redemption and Self-Deception." *Theology* 111.864 (Dec. 2008) 403–11.

Stedman, Ray C. *Hebrews*. The IVP New Testament Commentary Series. Downers Grove, IL: InterVarsity, 1992.

Strong, James. *The New Strong's Exhaustive Concordance of the Bible*. Nashville: Thomas Nelson, 1990.

Stulac, George M. *James*. The IVP New Testament Commentary Series. Downers Grove, IL: InterVarsity, 1993.

Sturm, Thomas. *Psychology's Territories: Historical and Contemporary Perspectives from Different Disciplines*. Edited by Mitchell G. Ash and Thomas Sturm. London: Lawrence Erlbaum Associates, 2007.

Ten Elshof, Gregg. *I Told Me So: Self-Deception and the Christian Life*. Grand Rapids: Eerdmans, 2009.

Thiselton, Anthony C. *The First Epistle to the Corinthians: A Commentary on the Greek Text*. The New International Greek Testament Commentary. Grand Rapids: Eerdmans, 2000.

Thompson, J. A. *The Book of Jeremiah*. The New International Commentary on the Old Testament. Grand Rapids: Eerdmans, 1980.

Via, Dan O. "The Gospel of Matthew: Hypocrisy as Self-Deception." In *Society of Biblical Literature 1988 Seminar Papers*, edited by David J. Lull, 508–16. Atlanta, GA: Scholars Press, 1988.

———. *Self-Deception and Wholeness in Paul and Matthew*. Eugene, OR: Wipf & Stock, 2005.

Wallace, Daniel B. *Greek Grammar beyond the Basics: An Exegetical Syntax of the New Testament*. Grand Rapids: Zondervan, 1996.

Bibliography

Waltke, Bruce. *The Book of Proverbs Chapters 1–15*. The New International Commentary on the Old Testament. Grand Rapids: Eerdmans, 2004.

———. *Genesis: A Commentary*. Grand Rapids: Zondervan, 2001.

Wenham, Gordon J. *Genesis 1–15*. Word Biblical Commentary 1. Waco, TX: Word Books, 1987.

Witherington, Ben, III. *Grace in Galatia: A Commentary on Paul's Letter to the Galatians*. Grand Rapids: Eerdmans, 1998.

Wood, Allen W. "Self-Deception and Bad Faith." In *Perspectives on Self-Deception*, edited by Brian P. McLaughlin and Amelie O. Rorty, 207–27. Berkeley: University of California Press, 1988.

Wood, William D. "Axiology, Self-Deception, and Moral Wrongdoing in Blaise Pascal's 'Pensées.'" *Journal of Religious Ethics* 37.2 (June 1, 2009) 355–84.

———. *Blaise Pascal on Duplicity, Sin and the Fall: The Secret Instinct*. Oxford: Oxford University Press, 2013.

———. "Searching for the Secret Instinct: Blaise Pascal and the Philosophical Analysis of Self-Deception." PhD diss., University of Chicago, 2007.

Wright, N. T. *Galatians*. Commentaries for Christian Formation. Grand Rapids: Eerdmans, 2021.

www.ingramcontent.com/pod-product-compliance
Lightning Source LLC
Chambersburg PA
CBHW072145160426
43197CB00012B/2248